CRYPTOCURRENCY INVESTING

Blockchain Revolution 2022

The Best strategies To Become a Crypto Millionaire

WARREN MEYERS

WARREN MEYERS ACADEMY

Acknowledgment

I want to thank you for buying my book and for the trust, sincerely ...Thanks!

Writing a book is harder than I thought and more rewarding than I could have ever imagined.

My thanks go to all of you, readers, I thank you because without you I could not be what I am, without you my books simply…would not exist!

I would like to invite you to know all my books and audiobooks that I have written and if you like my works, please, leave a positive tought, this will help me to move on on my work and will help other people to buy what they are find!

Again…Thanks You!

Warren Ramsey

Warren Meyers

Find my Books and my Audiobooks

Cryptocurrency Investing

Copyright 2022 by Warrem Meyers
All rights reserved.

TABLE OF CONTENTS

INTRODUCTION

There are people who, thanks to trading, have changed their lives and the lives of many people who have believed in them. It is enough to mention the name of Warren Buffet or George Soros because dreams and visions begin to appearin the heads of many traders.

Trading success is achieved staying grounded.

Starting from this belief, I wrote this manual in a simple way with the aim of helping newbies to find the right way to be successful, but above all to find the right methods to avoid losing money, very often, saved with many sacrifices.

Trading is not synonymous with gambling. Cryptocurrencytradingis neither a game nor a hobby. Your approach must be extremely serious and disciplined, especially your attention must be paid to safeguarding the capital you decide to invest. Knowing your character, your fears, your goals, knowing how to use all this to your advantage, is certainly an added weapon.

CHAPTER ONE

BLOCKCHAIN

In recent years, you have surely noticed the term "blockchain" being pronounced with increasing frequency. It is understandable when you consider the fact that many individuals are comparing the importance of blockchain technology tothat of the World Wide Web in the 1990s.

But what is blockchain? How does it work? Above all, how can you position yourself to capitalize on this innovation that could offer a huge growth opportunity?

Blockchain

Put simply, we could define blockchain as a shared database, a digital ledger, an archive of financial transactions that are saved on multiple computers in different places.

The database grows steadily as new transactions are added, also called "blocks". This forms a continuous chain of data in which the records are public and verifiable. As there is no head office, it is more difficult to hack information as it exists in millions of different places.

There are three main technologies that combine together to create a blockchain. These include private key cryptography, a distribution network with a shared ledger, and an incentive to maintain network transactions, record keeping and security. These combine to make blockchain technology a decentralized, transparent and immutable system.

Decentralization

Most traditional forms of payment are centralized. For example, your bank stores your money and to pay someone else you will have to go through the bank. This has several weaknesses:

- all data is stored in one place, making it an easy target for hackers;

- if the centralized entity shuts down or becomes corrupted, no one has access to the information it holds.

In a decentralized system, such as that created with blockchain technology, information is not stored by a single entity. Everyone in the network owns the information and can access the history of transactions, but cannot modify it. This immutability is another fundamental pillar of blockchain technology.

Immutability

Once something has been placed on the blockchain it cannot be tampered with. There is no possible way to "tinker" with the registers. This is because the underlying technology uses cryptographic hashes. In the context of payments, this means that transactions are taken as inputs and passed through a hashing algorithm that gives them an output of fixed length and size. This means that each hash can identify a very large set of calculations or a string of data.

Transparency

Perhaps the most interesting aspect of how blockchain works is the fact that it offers a high level of transparency and privacy at the same time. A user's identity is hidden behind complex encryption and can only be identified by their public address.

At the same time, while the user's identity is secure, one can still see all the transactions that have been made on his public address. This level of transparency does not exist in the current financial system and that is why blockchain technology is changing the world of finance, as we will see later in this article.

How does it work

Let's supposethatDavid wants to send Paul some money. Using blockchain technology this transaction would be represented online as a block. This block would be distributed across the blockchain network which is a special type of peer-to-peer network where the workload is partitioned among the participants rather than a central server.

Once the network verifies that the transaction is valid, the block is added to the chain and reconciled across the network, creating a permanent record. David's record of ownership of money then passes to Paul. In essence, the technology helps to cut the middleman out, but with full transparency and privacy.

How it works in the real world

One of the first real-world uses of this technology was in cryptographies like Bitcoin and Ethereum. This is due to the fact that technology allows digital information to be distributed and not copied, which means that each data can have only one owner which is essential when it comes to payments; in fact, a digital master book.

How Blockchain Works for Bitcoin

In 2008, someone using the pseudonym Satoshi Nakamoto created Bitcoin. Since the Bitcoin blockchain is decentralized, it is not controlled by a single central authority, unlike traditional currencies which are issued by a central bank. Instead, the Bitcoin blockchain is maintained by a network of miners (sometimes called "nodes"). These nodes are custom built computers that solve complex mathematical problems to get the transaction through.

Let'simagine that Davidmakes a Bitcoin transaction. This transaction would originate from David's digital currency wallet which will be protected by a private key. This key is nothing more than a digital signature from David, which provides mathematical proof that the transaction comes from that wallet.

If more people make more transactions, they will all be grouped into a block that will be organized by strict cryptographic rules. This block will then be sent to the Bitcoin network and once validated it will be added to the previous blocks, thus creating a chain of blocks.

Although this mightseem like a very long and convoluted way to make a transaction, keep in mind that all of these transactions are transparent and listed on the Bitcoin ledger (which you can search using a Bitcoin explorer). Furthermore, multiple parties need to authenticate the transaction and even if one part of the network were to collapse, the whole network would not collapse.

How Blockchain Works for Ethereum

Following the hype and the success of Bitcoin, a number of other companies have begun building platforms with blockchains that have been easier to use in the real world and by businesses. The second largest digital currency in the world by value- after Bitcoin - is Ethereum. It is essentially a blockchain platform that specializes in smart contracts and is linked to a digital currency called "Ether".

Ethereum's blockchain is public, just like Bitcoin's, and it allows people to build decentralized applications on its platform, which specializes in smart contracts. These are contracts that are automatically executed when certain conditions are met by all interested parties. This level of automation helps speed up the process.

How the wallet works

A blockchain wallet is nothing more than a software program that allows users to buy, sell and monitor their balance sheets with digital currencies such as Bitcoin and Ethereum. It is important to note that a blockchain wallet does not store cryptocurrencies. It simply keeps a record of all currency related transactions (your public and private keys) and stores them on the blockchain.

There are several types of block chain wallets available. Hardware wallets are hardware devices such as USB sticks that store private keys for a user. There are also software wallets, such as desktop, online and mobile applications, which store private keys for transactions made.

Blockchain technology itself, its uses and the services surrounding it are big business. It is the reason why many large companies are investing billions of dollars in its development. However, there are some blockchain stocks that stand out from others.

Before delving into this topic, you need to learn more or improve your knowledge of blockchain technology andbetter understand how to use blockchain.

How to invest in blockchain

To demonstrate how many investors are interested in blockchain stocks, just take a look at Riot Blockchain. It was a penny stock that went from just $8 per share to $40 per share in 2017 when they changed their name from Bioptix Inc to Riot Blockchain.

The company was a manufacturer of diagnostic machinery for the biotech industry. After changing its name and changing its brand to have a focus on buying cryptocurrency and blockchain assets, the shares have skyrocketed on investor hype. Over time, the company was investigated by the Securities and Exchange Commission.

This is an example of why investors need to do their research before buying the potential of blockchain technology. However, there are some well-known large companies that are investing billions in technology that all traders should be aware of.

The 3 Best Sharesfor 2020

According to a report by the World Economic Forum, about 10% of the world's gross domestic product (GDP) will likely be stored in blocks by 2027. Companies at the forefront of providing blockchain-powered services will be at the top of investor lists for 2020 and well beyond. Below you can find a list of just 3 stocks that can get you started and understand how to invest in blockchain, and that most investors may find interesting for 2020 and afterward.

IBM

IBM is one of the leaders in the development of blockchain technology. The company is supported by more than 1,500 industry experts, participating in more than 500 blockchain projects. One such project is the IBM Food Trust platform which was launched with Walmart in 2018. The goal was to improve food safety processes through an integrated supply-side blockchain.

According to Forbes, IBM " may be the largest and most successful of the blockchain companies". One reason is that the company helped create Hyperledger Fabric, after donating 44,000 lines of code to the project that formed the core of a new blockchain with faster speeds and greater privacy. Hyperledger Fabric is the gold standard for enterprise blockchain projects.

Over the past seven years, the IBM stock price has suffered from the lack of innovation of their counterparts like Microsoft and Apple. However, it is firmly at the heart of blockchain development, and investors will be on the lookout for signals that help achieve the company's bottom line and mark a turn in the fortune of its share price.

In the long-term monthly chart of the IBM stock price, the downward trend from mid-2013 to the end of 2018 is evident. The coronavirus pandemic has made its effects felt, but IBM appears to be recovering and investors will now be interested to see if the IBM share price will manage to increase its momentum during 2020. Blockchain technology is new, but it helps to be at the heart of its development.

Alibaba

Alibaba is China's largest e-commerce and technology company. In November, Ant Financial, the fintech arm of the Alibaba Group, launched the test phase for its blockchain network aimed at supporting small and medium-sized businesses.

The group has also started a partnership with the Chinese government for the use of blockchains in the healthcare sector. The Chinese government has already announcedthatit wants to be a world leader in blockchain technology, and Alibaba looks set to take advantage of this, as it has not only built a large blockchain patent library, but is already using the technology in its subsidiary and e-commerce Lynx and T-Mall, winning a practical and real advantage.

On the long-term weekly chart of the Alibaba stock price, it is clear that the company has done well - even before excelling in adopting blockchain technology. The success of its e-commerce platform offers great support to investors who still distrust the potential of blockchain. The coronavirus pandemic, on the other hand, appears to have favored Alibaba thanks to the increase in online orders as a result; combined with the success in both areas it could be a powerful driver of Alibaba's share price throughout 2020 and afterward.

MasterCard

Mastercard ranks third in the world among the best blockchain innovators with over 100 blockchain patents filed. The company's advancement in blockchain technology is interesting as the technology itself is designed to make centralized intermediaries obsolete.

However, the company is using the technology to reduce transaction costs and increase fraud protection. With over $21 billion in fraud losses suffered by banks in 2015, there is a huge advantage in using technology that allows transparency and privacy at the same time, in addition to its immutability.

The way Mastercard has approached blockchain technology is evident of an innovative and forward-thinking company that shareholders and investors will be pleased with.

The long-term monthly chart of the Mastercard stock price shows a very impressive upward trend. The share price is trading at a high level, and has been doing so since 2006. How the company has adapted to this new technology that threatens parts of its business could mean that the upward trend is here to stay.

CHAPTER TWO

ICO

Anyone who has the slightest familiarity with the world of cryptocurrencies, has at least once heard of ICOs (Initial Coin Offering).

This is a fundraiser aimed at collecting economic resources for those start-ups that develop projects in the blockchain field. ICOs exploded in 2017 only to have a big drop in 2018.

At the moment, they almost seem to have been replaced by IEOs.

Currently, it is no longer possible to invest directly in ICOs.

To better understand what ICOs are, just think that it is the acronym of Initial Coin Offering.

How they worked was not too different from IPOs that take place on the stock market and have the same purpose.

A start-up that operates on the blockchain, in fact, decides to take the big step going public, or opening up to investors.

The ICOs made it possible to obtain the necessary funds to continue their projects. Unlike a regular crowdfunding campaign, however, ICOs offered investors a real advantage.

Investors, in fact, were rewarded in tokens. As we will see, these are cryptocurrency units issued by the start up and given as a reward to investors during the ICO.

In this way the start-up receives funds and the investors, instead, receive tokens which, if the project of the financed company goes through, will be worth much more than what was paid.

Obviously the advantage of ICOs lay in the fact that, if you could evaluate a start-up well, the profits that could be obtained were enormous.

Differences Between IPO and ICO

Let's go into more detail, recalling other important differences between IPO and ICO.

The main one concerns the fact that, in ICOs, unlike what happens with IPOs, the company that initiates the fundraising is not required to meet particular criteria.

Virtually anyone can open a fundraiser for a blockchain-related project.

Warning: this does not mean that all ICOs are destined for success. Many of them, in fact, start and fail after a short time.

The lack of proper regulation of ICOs has caused their decline. To date, in fact, it is no longer possible to participate in these collections.

Alternatives to ICOs

Normally, when an ICO was launched, participants were rewarded in tokens or cryptocurrencies.

Conceptually, the ICO is very similar to the IPO of the equity world. Everything, however, takes place on the blockchain in a decentralized manner.

Most of the people who wanted to make money from ICOs understood today that the best way remains to speculate on virtual currencies.

Today, when this tool is no longer available, many investors have nonetheless grasped the basic principle and found an alternative way to earn from emerging cryptocurrencies.

How to invest in ICOs: White Papers

Everything about investing in ICOs was extremely complex.

When approaching emerging cryptocurrencies in general, in fact, it is necessary, as already mentioned, to remember that not all projects are valid.

In any case, it is good to specify that protections existed and still exist.

In fact, every single ICO had to present a specific prospectus, technically known as a WhitePaper.

For the sake of completeness, it must be remembered that the White Papers are not subject to the control of external bodies.

In light of this aspect, it is not uncommon for them to highlight above all the positive and advantageous aspects of the project. This is why the sector has been closed to the public of retail traders.

Crucially, in spite of everything, it was vital that you read it carefully before joining any ICO.

There were some aspects to pay particular attention to when reading the WhitePaper of an ICO and that can help you, today, to understand how to evaluate a young cryptocurrency.

In this category, it is possible to include information about the people behind the project (previous experiences in other similar projects in the first place), but also everything related to competitors.

ICO rewards the tokens

In the previous lines we mentioned that, when participating in an ICO, it was possible to be rewarded in different ways. One of these is token distribution.

These are "tokens" which, in the case of ICOs in the crypto world, correspond to a certain amount of the future cryptocurrency.

Going deeper, we also find different types of tokens.

Here's what they are:

<u>Equity tokens</u>

These tokens are similar to the shares of companies listed on regulated markets. Whoever owns them can claim a right towards the start-up that issued them. Right now, this type of token cannot be issued for reasons of legality. The current legislation, in fact, assimilates equity tokens to shares.

Utility tokens: in this case, we are dealing with tokens that have nothing to do with the world of stocks. This means that they can be traded on the markets and used within the various platforms.

Do you want to make money with cryptocurrencies, but you don't know where to start or are you confused with all the information you find on the net?

A very important parenthesis when talking about what ICOs are concerns the analysis of regulations.

Token class 2 a

Class 2 a tokens are representative of assets and entitle you to a specific payment both at sight and in the future.

Depending on its configuration, the token can be classified in the context of securities, but also in that of similar or financial instruments.

Furthermore, the class 2 a token can be included in the category of equity instruments

Token class 2 b

First of all, remember that, in this case, we are dealing with tokens aimed at providing services or receiving intangible assets.

It happens that the discipline of the ICO loses all the connotations of the offer of financial instruments. In practice, in the initial phase of the ICO, various advantages are highlighted, dedicated to users who acquire the tokens first.

<u>Token class 3</u>

We are dealing with tokens that confer co-ownership rights. The aforementioned rights are managed by the platforms themselves.

In these situations, the owner is given an economic compensation following the use of the platforms by a third party.

Stop ICOs with online trading

The halt to ICO investments came from September 2017. The Popular Bank of China's decision to shut down the ICO market in China has led to a chain reaction.

Leading financial authorities around the world have gone to great lengths to issue stringent industry regulations. Among these also the ESMA (European Security and Markets Authority), with two press releases of November 2017.

Don't get us wrong, ICOs haven't been made completely illegal. However, there have been many in the following years, but the policy on risk prevention in online trading has led to making them inaccessible to retail traders like you.

Investing in ICOs today is no longer safe as it is a possibility that is no longer offered to you by the main online trading platforms.

Successful ICO

To fully understand the peculiarities of ICOs, it is appropriate to call into question some successful examples.

Let's start with thatof Ethereum. To do this, we have to take a step back to 2013. In that year, the very young VitalikButerin launched a 42-day ICO, with the aim of financing the Ethereum project.

What were the results? A gain of 31,591 Bitcoins, corresponding to approximately 18 million US dollars.

In 2018, other successful ones were also launched. Among these, it is possible to remember the Cypherium project, promoted and carried out by professionals with experience in Amazon, Google and Microsoft.

In this case, we are dealing with a project that has a completely new blockchain as its goal. Specifically, we are dealing with a multi-level governance that, according to some, could lead to a new decentralization in the world of cryptocurrencies.

To mention, when talking about the successful ICOs of recent times, is also the LociCoin project.

What is it about? An ICO launched with thegoalof creating a cryptocurrencyfor the purchase of intellectual rights.

The project in question aims to streamline the process of acquiring patents, which are now subject to both national and international rules that are often excessively rigid.

Most successful ICOs: how much did they raise?

To make you understand how much money has been invested in ICOs, take a look at some of them:

Telegram Open Network - $1.7 billion;

Dragon Coin - $320 million;

Huobi - $300 million;

HDac - $258 million;

Filecoin - $257 million;

Tezos - $232 million;

Sirin Labs - $157.9 million;

Bancor - $152 million.

The list could go on and on!

We will limit ourselves to mention the example of CoinLancer, a project that aims to improve the freelance world lowering transaction fees.

We conclude talking about Omega One, a project that intendsto solve the defects of ICOs, intervening on problems such as lack of liquidity and attacks by computer hackers.

CHAPTER THREE

IEO

What is an IEO

An Initial Exchange Offering (IEO) is a token sale supervised by a cryptocurrency exchange. IEOs are available exclusively to exchange users, although some IEOs may occur on some exchanges. Just like ICOs, IEOs allow investors to obtain new cryptocurrencies (or tokens) while raising funds for promising crypto projects.

Many people in the crypto world call Initial Exchange Offerings the next step in the evolution of ICOs. Since ICOs are unregulated and most of them turned out to be scams, STOs should have solved the problem. However, most STOs remain constrained by slow and expensive processes and suffocating regulations. IEOs are the middle ground that tackles problems on both sides.

Although exchange-assisted ICOs have been something worthwhile for some time, IEOs started gaining ground after the launch of the Binance Launchpad in late 2018. There have already been more than 50 IEOs in 2019, which have garnered over $159 million, according to ICObench.

IEOs try to promote only legitimate projects because they challenge the credibility of the exchange itself. Therefore, the control process goes deeper. However, not all ideas manage to get support from an exchange. Additionally, exchange offerings are more accessible than STOs, as they allow almost anyone to participate and invest (except for countries with regulatory restrictions, see below), and the token sales team is less likely to be impacted by lawmakers due to the mandatory KYC/AML control of investors, as this service is performed by the exchange.

Essentially, the IEO is another way to crowdfund for various cryptocurrency startups through a crypto exchange that acts as a broker. With the help of the crypto exchange, projects are able to gain significantly more exposure, interest and credibility.

After an initial phase with a successful IEO, the token issuer pays a commission due to the established amount of tokens for making use of the services offered by the IEO platform. Quickly the tokens are listed on the exchange where investors can access instant liquidity.

Characteristics of Initial Exchange Offerings (IEO)

As with ICOs, IEOs have a limited amount of coins offered at a fixed price, limits on the minimum and maximum number of tokens that the individual user can purchase, soft caps and hard caps and the specific cryptocurrencies that are accepted.

However, unlike ICO tokens, IEO coins are already mined before the crowdsale. Furthermore, they enter exchanges several days or weeks after its IEO, which makes it more convenient for investors (immediate liquidity). Furthermore, the IEO process naturally involves an intermediary (the IEO platform) who is trusted to manage the funds. This also serves to increase investor confidence, which is lacking in most ICOs.

Pros and Cons of IEOs

IEOs are essentially advantageous thanks to:

- greater investor confidence.

- In fact the investors are not dealing with the IEO project team directly, but with the exchange. This makes the whole process more credible and safer in case things go wrong;

- security for both token issuers and investors.

- Token issuers also gain as IEO platforms handle all regulatory aspects, such as the mandatory KYC/AML checks for each participant;

- frictionless process.

- IEO platforms ensure that almost anyone, regardless of their experience in the crypto world, can easily contribute;

- guaranteed exchange listing. IEO tokens are listed on the IEO exchange right after the IEO;

- scam removal.

- IEO project teams are neither anonymous nor fake, so they won't disappear after raising the funds;

- benefits for projects, such as greater marketing effort by the exchange, more credibility, more exposure and interest in the project;

- benefits for exchnage, including new users who sign up with them only to buy and trade IEO tokens;

- benefits for holders of native exchangetokens.

- Most exchanges use IEOs to add another use case to their native token (if it has one) which is then likely to increase in value.

However, IEOs are also subject to the following risks and concerns:

- unclear regulations and restrictions.

- Many countries have issued restrictions or completely banned ICOs, which could reflect negatively on IEOs as well. Although it is slightly different, the fundamental principles of an IEO remain the same;

- all investors must comply with AML/KYC.

- The crypto community is known to be full of privacy

obsessed people, so going through the AML/KYCprocess might be a big no-no for some of them;

- market manipulation and coin concentration.

- Most IEO tokens are mined early, so you should always double-check your token distribution and allocation details before investing. Both the project team and the IEO exchange could keep an unreasonably large portion of the tokens for themselves, which could lead to pricing meddling later on. Furthermore, it is now known that the majority of exchanges participate in "wash trading";

- limited number of investors.

- There have been a lot of complaints from investors that not everyone is able to buy tokens during IEO sessions.

The first large-scale IEO was famously thatof BitTorrent launched by TRON through the Binance Launchpad in January 2019. About 60 billion BTT tokens were sold in a few minutes for a total of about 7.2 million USD.

After observing the success of Binance's IEOs, major exchanges have started copying the model. Another notable IEO was launched on Bittrex International. Veriblock (VBK) and raised $7 million in 10.4 seconds. Later, this record was surpassed by the IEO Blockcloud operated on OKEx's Jumpstart, which sold all $2.5 million in BLOC tokens in just one second.

CHAPTER FOUR

DIGITAL TOKEN

A token is a set of digital information within a blockchain that confers a right on a particular subject, tokenization is the conversion of the rights of an asset into a digital token registered on a blockchain.

One of the words that recur most frequently when talking about the new economy and blockchain is certainly that of token. However, not everyone knows that two distinct meanings and aswell asmany peculiarities can be attributed to the term token, depending on the context in which this term is used.

The Token in Cryptocurrencies

Obviously, the sector to which reference is made to attribute a first meaning of token is that of cryptocurrencies, in fact starting from the assumption that a cryptocurrency is an "electronic money" (even if here the meaning of currency should certainly be deepened, but only for simplification it is defined as such) based on blockchain or other distributed ledger, we can certainly say that each of these cryptocurrencies (Bitcoin, Ethereum etc.) has its own transaction register on which exchanges are stored. Tokensare in fact fractions of an issued cryptocurrency, which are exchanged between users through exchanges that are stored on the aforementioned register. To simplify, this type of "token" should be defined as "coin",a term that although it indicates the same concept (when we refer to cryptovalue or a fraction of it), in reality, is less confusing.

There is in fact another type of "token" also called token, which unlike those mentioned above, does not have its own register, but uses the register of another coin. For example, through Ethereum's smart contracts, anyone can issue their own tokens, evenwith an ICO (Initial Coin Offer) and record the transactions relating to that token on the Ethereum blockchain instead of necessarily building their own. These "tokens" acquire the unique token appellation.

The token therefore has the same characteristics as the cryptocurrency (security and non-censurable transferability) but is not "native" and above all "internal" to the blockchain on which the transactions concerning it are stored but represents the digital twin of a real asset, a right "real", but which exists outside the blockchain system.

A further difference is expressed in the fact that the issuance of tokens (tokens that do not have their own blockchain) is not particularly complicated:essentially it is enough to write a smart contract on the mainnet of another coin, for example the Ethereum network. The creation of a new coin, on the other hand, is a much more complex process, as it is necessary to develop a new protocol, create the mainnet, make sure you have a sufficiently powerful hardware to make it "run" and above all hopingthat someone will use it.

Hoping to have clarified this first difference and focused attention on the term token intended as a token created using a blockchain of an existing coin, we can certainly say that a token is a set of digital information within a blockchain that confers a right to a particular subject. Consequently, tokenization is the conversion of the rights of an asset into a digital token registered on a blockchain, where the real asset and the token are connected by a smart contract. Therefore tokenizing means generating a token in the virtual world and connecting it to an existing asset in the real world through the use of smart contracts.

What is "tokenizable"

Theoretically, anything can be tokenizable, so much that in the not too distant future we hope and expect a real revolution comparable to what was the advent of the internet in our society: in fact, the blockchain promises to revolutionize not only all aspects directly linked to finance, but also public and civil services. It is likely that we will soon live in a fully tokenized economy, where every form of value storage and public recording will be represented by a token.

Currently, several sectors are experimenting with tokenization, which has already been implemented not only in the real estate sector (with luxury condominiums enabled for tokenization on Ethereum) but also in sectors such as works of art and sports. The strength of the tokenization of an asset lies in the fact that it is possible to make liquid assets otherwise indivisible, to manage assets plastered by excessive bureaucracy through the concrete implementation of the concept of "democratization" of the shareholding. Not only that, it is possible to digitize anything exploiting the flexibility and security of the token to implement a series of previously unthinkable commercial initiatives. In the real estate sector, for example, the purchase of a small fraction of a property also allows small investors to enter a market that is usually closed to them, without resorting to mortgages and intermediaries from credit institutions. For manufacturers, the advantage of this type of financing is to offer greater flexibility and capital inflows in the short term.

Same concept for the tokenization of some works of art, where participants in special auctions received digital shares of the work. Also in the world of sport, some companies have decided to manage business decisions through decentralized platforms that allow the sale of shares and rights to fans around the world quickly and safely, giving fans the advantage of being able to access exclusive content and services.

In other sectors, its products are being tokenized creating special rewards consisting of tokens to encourage purchases and retain customers.

Token, stock exchange and circular economy

The use of computer tokens is also very useful in the stock market sector. There are already projects for the tokenization of "stock exchanges" with the development of decentralized platforms, or infrastructures for the exchange of shares, thus protecting them from manipulations other than the "natural" ones of the market. To encourage projects of this type, the tokenization of company shares has begun to be evaluated.

Another fundamental aspect of tokenization is the absolute predisposition of this revolution to the creation of a circular economy. It is now known that the linear economic model "production-consumption-waste" which is based on the use of large quantities of resources and energy with relative waste of materials that can easily be put back into circulation, is less and less in line with today's reality,and will necessarily have to transform itself into an economy capable of being able to self-regenerate, and the use of tokens and the tokenization process represents the perfect case use.

CHAPTER FIVE

START INVESTING IN CRYPTOCURRENCIES

For several years, virtual currencies such as Bitcoin have been recognized as an essential and very attractive investment vehicle for investors.

The volatility of cryptocurrencies offers traders numerous trading opportunities. Therefore, digital currencies have become increasingly popular in trading strategies in orderto diversify their investment portfolio.

Today, in 2020, there are two ways to invest in cryptocurrencies:

- buying cryptocurrencies on an exchange platform to hold them in an online or offline cryptocurrency wallet;

- trading these financial assets via CFDs directly on a trading platform

Cryptocurrency Trading and Cryptocurrency Trading Strategies.

But what exactly sets a successful cryptocurrency trader apart from other investors?

And more importantly, how do you need to prepare to take on these financial markets and become a successful cryptocurrency trader?

Investing in Cryptocurrencies

What is a cryptocurrency

Despite being a global phenomenon, cryptocurrencies are sometimes difficult to understand, however their definition is relatively simple.

A cryptocurrency is a 100%, fully decentralized digital currency that is only traded in pairs. All validated cryptocurrency transactions are recorded on what is called the blockchain.

The principle of a cryptocurrency is to provide a monetary alternative for people looking to regain control of their money becoming their own bank. Some properties of cryptocurrencies are revolutionary.

Among the features of these 2.0 currencies, decentralization and peer-to-peer exchanges allow their users to not trust their money towards banks and to carry out transactions without intermediaries.

Therefore, central bodies no longer have control of the change in the money supply (inflation vs. deflation). Furthermore, they cannot refuse or cancel a transaction or block funds, as they have no power over cryptocurrencies.

Investingin Cryptocurrencies With CFDs

Unlike cryptocurrency exchange platforms that allow you to trade your dollars for cryptocurrencies and then keep them as long as you want in your virtual wallet, the benefits of investing in cryptocurrencies with CFDs are greater, especially for those who want to take advantage of rapid price changes.

CFD stands for"Contract For Difference" and is a type of derivative product. Therefore, it is a financial instrument whose valuation depends on another instrument called an "underlying".

Using a CFD, you never own the underlying instrument, asyou are only investing in the price change between the opening and closing of the contract.

Advantages of trading cryptocurrencies via CFDs

- Bullish and bearish investments: you can make money as cryptocurrency prices rise and fall

- Leverage:take advantage of margin and leverage which increase market exposure

- High volatility: maximizes the volatility of the cryptocurrency market

- Better liquidity: get better prices and shorter execution times that allow you to increase performance through better liquidity

- Reduction of the risk of loss, theft and cyber attacks related to storing your cryptocurrencies in a wallet, since you don't have tokens that use CFDs

- Flexible trading hours: trade on a 24-hour market

- Regulated and safe environment: benefit from a safe and regulated business environment with protections as a private operator, such as negative balance protection

- Low starting capital required: start trading cryptocurrency CFDs with relatively low capital

Disadvantages of trading cryptocurrency with CFDs

- You do not actually own cryptocurrencies: you do not have cryptocurrencies since you use CFDs on cryptocurrencies

- Leverage: you need to master leverage. Traders risk losing their deposit faster when using leverage, so use it with caution

- High volatility: the volatility of cryptocurrency prices is high. It is for this reason that we need to understand the concept of volatility and integrate it into a rigorous trading plan

Characteristics of Virtual Cryptocurrencies

There are no coins or bills. Everything is on the Internet and on computers

Like any other currency, a cryptocurrency can be used to make purchases when accepted by merchants, to send money to someone, to receive money, etc.

Decentralized

There is no government or country that controls cryptocurrencies unlike traditional currencies.

The total money supply of a cryptocurrency is often limited. In this case, it is determined at the time of creation of the cryptocurrency and indicated in its technical document. The bitcoin money supply, for example, is not expected to exceed 21 million BTC tokens.

Without intermediaries

To execute a transaction with a cryptocurrency, it is not necessary to use a trusted third party such as a bank or other intermediary to validate it. Transactions are carried out on a peer-to-peer basis via electronic wallets that are carried out in applications to buy cryptocurrencies, websites or even exchange platforms.

Based on blockchain

Traditional currencies under the control of central banks such as the Fed (Federal Reserve) for the US dollar (USD) or the ECB (European Central Bank) for the euro (EUR).

In the case of cryptocurrencies, all transactions are performed on the blockchain, which acts as a large, transparent and tamper-proof accounting book open to all.

Encrypted

The term "cryptocurrency" comes from the principle that it is an encrypted currency. It can only be used by the person with the decryption code that allows, for example, the use of cryptocurrencies in a wallet.

Safe

Since the funds use an advanced cryptographic system with a combination of public/private keys, your funds are safe. Furthermore, the blocks that belong to the blockchain (those that group all validated transactions) are linked together by complex computer formulas that avoid any data manipulation.

Fast

Validating the blockchain transaction is much faster than most traditional operators such as Visa or SWIFT. Some transactions are validated almost instantly.

Irreversible

Once a transaction involving cryptocurrencies is confirmed, it is no longer possible to withdraw. Therefore, it is impossible to cancel a transaction if a cryptocurrency transfer has failed or your tokens have been stolen.

(Pseudo) Anonymous

Depending on the cryptocurrency you use, you can enjoy a greater or lesser degree of anonymity.

Even if you receive cryptocurrencies at encrypted addresses that don't directly reflect your identity in the real world, once you share this address with someone to receive funds, that person can see all the movements taking place in that direction.

CHAPTER SIX

INVESTING IN CRYPTOCURRENCIES SUCCESSFULLY

Success in trading can take on different meanings for every trader who has decided to invest in cryptocurrencies.

For some, being successful could mean making a profit on a real trading account or demo trading from the 30 minute chart. For others, it could mean making a profit from a short position in cryptocurrency CFDs. Ultimately, however, success most likely comes down to a profitable return on the capital that everyone has invested and therefore exposed to risk.

Of course, as with any other business, the tools we use will have an impact on our overall success. After all, no one wants to spend a great deal of time researching and analyzing a trading opportunity with a high probability of success, only to end up with a platform that is either unresponsive or suffering from the technical issues that prevent them from completing the strategy.

Here are some of the fundamental tools for increasing the odds of long-term success as a cryptocurrency trader.

Choose a trusted broker

Those who decide to physically purchase a cryptocurrency will have to do so through a cryptocurrency exchange system. These are often unregulated entities that are prone to attacks. For example:

In 2018, Japan's Coincheck was hacked and more than $500 million worth of digital currency was stolen.

In 2017, Youbit - a South Korean stock exchange - had to close and declare bankruptcy after being hacked twice.

In 2014, MtGox - a Japanese exchange that handled nearly 80% of all global Bitcoin transactions - closed after 850,000 Bitcoins disappeared from its virtual vaults (worth around half a billion dollars at the time).

Even when it comes to CFDs, the broker with whom you decide to invest in cryptocurrencies holds the capital with which you will then have to trade. Therefore, it is important to choose an entity that offers the highest possible regulatory oversight, safety and assurance.

The trading platform

Your trading platform and charts help you visualize the historical price movements of the financial instrument you are trading, as well as provide you with the orders you need to place and manage your trades. Some people may have a separate charting platform from their brokerage platform. With the new and advanced trading technology, however, it is now possible to have the trading platform and brokerage platform in one software with the MetaTrader product suite.

The trading strategy

Trading is all about making decisions about how to buy, sell, or sit idle on a particular market. If a trader has been successful over a substantial period of time there will be a greater chance that they are using a trading strategy or methodology to help in their decision making. Trading strategies are used to help simplify the information process which can include when to trade and when not to trade, what times to focus on, which technical indicators to use, how to enter and exit, and so on.

Of course, the tools used will depend on the trading styleof each one. This is the first thing to establish when starting to invest in cryptocurrencies. After all, if your goal is to trade cryptocurrency CFDs from the hourly chart, which involves multiple buying and selling throughout the day for short-term profits and closing positions at the end of the day, using a weekly long termchart for price analysis can only prove to be of little use.

Trading styles generally incorporate one or both types of analysis:

- Technical analysis. This type of analysis involves analyzing the price movement of financial products, in this case of cryptocurrencies, to identify repeatable patterns of behavior. Many traders use technical indicators applied to cryptocurrencies to find clues and price levels in which the market may move.

- Fundamental analysis. It involves analyzing news announcements related to financial products, and in this caseto cryptocurrencies, such as the new developments and uses of the technology behind crypto, namely the blockchain.

There are also types of events that are uniquely related to cryptocurrencies, an example is the "halving", which we will explore further on.

Here are some trading styles that you can apply to invest in cryptocurrencies:

- day trading

  This style involves buying and selling in various trading positions several times a day, often closing all trades by the end of the day. Traders using this style mainly rely on technical analysis tools such as trading indicators and chart patterns in their trading decisions. Investing in cryptocurrencies is worthwhile when using this type of trading style, as intraday traders need to trade the right tools to profit from different types of market conditions, such as rising and falling markets;

- swing trading

  This style involves buying and selling financial assets

with the purpose of holding trades for several days and, in some cases, several weeks. Traders using this style of trading often use a mix of technical analysis and fundamental analysis, such as analyzing new developments in "blockchain"cryptocurrency technology, to aid in their trading decisions.

CHAPTER SEVEN

HOW TO TRADE CRYPTOCURRENCIES

A Few Steps to Facilitate the Process

Work on your trading plan

First of all, it is important to know what kind of trader you are to confirm that cryptocurrency CFDs are the products you need. Think about your personality, your financial goals, seed capital, risk tolerance and the time you are willing to devote to trading.

If trading cryptocurrencies through leveraged derivatives such as CFDs seems like a good option for short-term trading, it is essential to work on your trading plan, test and follow it at all times.

A trading plan is simply a detailed description of how you will conduct your business: style, strategy to follow, risk management, objectives, etc.

Therefore, the idea is to develop a number of rules to follow in order to better manage operations. Therefore, you will avoid operating spontaneously without any strategy.

A trading plan is not a quick fix. Sometimes it takes time to develop a profitable trading strategy.

Don't forget also that some strategies only work in certain market situations, such as side consolidation or, conversely, in a market with a strong trend.

To tailor your trading plan, it may be worth keeping a trading journal and taking advantage of the option to trade virtual funds to practice.

Choose a broker with advantageous trading conditions and a trading account tailored to your needs

After designing your trading plan, you will have a more appropriate idea of your needs.

This will allow you to choose the correct platform and account type to start trading with a regulated broker that offers you the best trading conditions.

Without the right broker and trading platform, you will not be able to analyze or execute your trades quickly and correctly, which will affect your overall performance.

Start trading knowing how the market works

You can now start trading with cryptocurrencies! Here is an example of cryptocurrency trading that shows how much you can win or lose in one position.

Hypothesis:

Let's assume BTC/USD is the pair you want to trade with. Believe that Bitcoin has reached significant support and will recover soon. Therefore, open a position in the Bitcoin vs USD pair through a CFD to take advantage of the price increase.

For example: Bitcoin's bid/ask price, or "Bitcoin price", is 7000/7034. As a reminder, the selling price is always lower than the buying price. The difference between the two prices corresponds to the spread.

Therefore, you make a 1 contract buy/sell contract on the BTC/USD pair at $7000. Since the leverage is 1:2, this means that you need to set aside $3,500 (the margin) to open a buy position on a contract from 1 BTC/USD.

Winning position
========

Your ideal scenario is realized and the pair rises to reach the $7200 level. The new Bitcoin price is 7166/7200. Therefore, you decide to close the position (and thus sell) with a sell price of 7166.

Since the Bitcoin price at the time of purchase was 7000 and the price at the time of the sale was 7166, you took advantage of a $166 price shift. Therefore, your gross profit is $166 since you only opened one contract.

Losing position
========

Bitcoin's value does not appear to recover from the expected level and is accelerating downwards. You decide to close your position with a new price at the price of $6834/$6868.

Since the price of Bitcoin at the time of purchase was $7000 and the price at the time of the sale was $6834, you have lost $166. Therefore, the gross loss is $166 since you only opened one contract.

Check your money management

You are probably wondering why many traders lose money investing in cryptocurrencies. The answer is actually quite simple. They don't have a trading plan and don't use risk and money management tools to control their risk and protect their capital!

Therefore, risk and money management is essential if you want to be successful in long-term cryptocurrency trading while preserving your capital.

That is why it is important to always make sure that you manage risk as outlined in the trading plan. To be sure, it's important to always stick to your business plan. Also think about the following questions:

Do you use a risk/reward ratio to place stop-loss and take-profit orders that fit your strategy?

Do you risk more than 1% of your capital in one position?

Have you recently increased the size of your position just because you made some winning trades?

Do you have a well diversified portfolio?

Do you often deviate from your trading plan?

Follow cryptocurrency prices and market news

The most important thing in cryptocurrency trading is to always monitor your investments. Follow the cryptocurrency price in real time and market news. In fact, many movements in cryptocurrency quotes started with the "most popular" cryptocurrency news of the moment.

Discover the events that have the greatest influence on the price of cryptocurrencies

The cryptocurrency market is a new market whose fundamentals are still quite vague. This is why the greatest influence on prices continues to be the evolution of the relationship between supply and demand. Among the most influential factors for cryptocurrency prices are:

- market sentiment;

- news on cryptocurrency trading platforms;

- the evolution of the level of acceptance of cryptos;

- speed of execution and scalability of tokens and blockchains;

- the number of cryptocurrencies issued relative to the total money supply;

- the process of reducing miners' premiums (halving);

- cryptocurrency reputation.

<u>Best time to trade cryptocurrencies</u>

There really are no better times to trade in the cryptocurrency market. In fact, it never stops working. Therefore, every part of the world manages Bitcoin and the rest of the cryptocurrencies, which means that there will always be movements.

It can be interesting to trade when multiple exchanges are active, such as when European and American sessions are active. You can also trade at night and on weekends.

Mistakes to avoid whenstarting to invest in cryptocurrencies

- Don't define the trader's personality, risk profile and trading plan before starting to trade with real money

- Set unrealistic goals

- Don'tinvest in yourself (always try to improve knowledge through free cryptocurrency training)

- Trade an asset without knowing the details of the CFD

- Don't diversify your portfolio enough

- Don't accept you lose

- Lose patience

- Don't manage emotions

- Don't let your profits run and don't limit your losses

Which cryptocurrency to invest in 2020

Now that you know exactly what a cryptocurrency is and how it works, you are probably wondering which cryptocurrencies will be exploited in 2020 and in the coming years.

You must first understand that every cryptocurrency is different. Each of themhas its own advantages and challenges. Therefore, the best cryptocurrency to invest primarily depends on your goals in trading and your interest in cryptocurrency and what it contributes. Currencies that are already very popular often benefit from greater confidence and higher price movements than you can.

Future of Cryptocurrencies

The fall in cryptocurrencies after the peak in late 2017 led many people to believe it was the end of cryptocurrencies. But after several years, there are still many virtual currencies that currently offer attractive valuations.

The cryptocurrencies that will be exploited in 2020 should be small tokens that are not very popular (and often not available for trading) or major cryptocurrencies such as Bitcoin or Ethereum.

In any case, the most promising cryptocurrencies in 2020 are those that continue to evolve and offer more and more innovative features for their users.

The cryptocurrencies of the future must provide a real solution to the problems of legal currencies and an alternative to the challenges of our economy. It is also important that your adoption continues to support your development.

CHAPTER EIGHT

BITCOIN

Bitcoin is a digital currency, or "cryptocurrency", as it uses cryptography to secure transactions within its infrastructure, which represents a distributed online database, or "blockchain".

The abbreviation for Bitcoin is BTC. The same principle applies to USD (US dollar) and EUR (Euro).

Bitcoin can also be paired with other currencies. In that case, the name of the bitcoin CFD contract could be, for example, Bitcoin CFD against US dollar, or BTC/USD.

Bitcoin offers the opportunity to make fast, secure, low-cost peer-to-peer (P2P) payments without the need for a bank or central processor.

System transactions are performed directly between users' digital folders and are verified in the blockchain. Transactions are digitally signed with unique private keys, proving they come from the wallet owner.

History of Bitcoin

When a new block is created in the chain, it is rewarded with 12.5 Bitcoins. This happens approximately every 10 minutes.

This is a reward for the so-called "mining" process, which wastes electrical energy and computer power in maintaining the network.

Mining involves many people and specialized companies around the world and creates the core value of Bitcoin.

The system automatically generates new Bitcoins and self-regulates the speed of this process so that there is no way to circumvent global rules and earn Bitcoins faster than with investments in mining hardware and with higher spending on electricity bills.

The block reward will be halved in 2020 and will continue to be halved every 4 years until 21 million Bitcoins are generated. This means that Bitcoin has fundamental potential for value growth.

The image shows that there are more than 16 million (76% of the total) of Bitcoin on the market in 2018. The image also indicates rapid growth in its supply between the beginning of 2009 and 2013. We have seen that during 2018 the value of cryptocurrencies plummeted, so we need to be aware of the effect this can have on their demand.

Who invented Bitcoin

Bitcoin is believed to have been created by Satoshi Nakamoto, who announced its invention on October 31, 2008 on an encrypted mailing list in a research paper called Bitcoin: A Peer to Peer Electronic Box System. What's more interesting is that its name is likely a pseudonym used by the unknown, or by the people who originally designed Bitcoin. In 2016, Craig Wright, an Australian businessman, declared himself "Mr. Bitcoin", a statementthat has been widely accepted by prominent members of the Bitcoin community.

Bitcoin's financial history dates back to 2010, May 22, 2010, when someone bought a pizza. If you haven't heard of this groundbreaking event, don't worry, you're not the only one.

The pizza wasn't the most important part of the transaction - but what was used to pay for it. The meal cost 10,000 Bitcoins: it was the first time this virtual currency was used to buy something in the real world.

The day is now celebrated by Bitcoin enthusiasts every year as Bitcoin Pizza Day.

Things have changed since then. Bitcoin's use and value have skyrocketed. If that pizzeria had taken over those 10,000 Bitcoins, it might not have made history, but today it would have around $20 million in its pocket.

There are a lot of things you can buy using Bitcoin - besides pizza. There are even more places that accept it. According to www.coindesk.com, the number of merchants accepting Bitcoin has exploded. Many of them are online e-commerce sites, but a growing number of offline stores also accept BTC. The list is constantly expanding, and you will be able to spend bitcoins literally anywhere.

Common household items:

- video games;

- gift cards;

- travels;

- food;

- car;

- tips and charity;

- online and offline stores.

Most Bitcoin payment processors will also provide a QR code on the box, which represents the address and amount of the Bitcoin payment.

QR codes are very convenient, so it's easy to pay through the Bitcoin wallet application from your smartphone. Just scan the QR code and enter the recipient's Bitcoin address and the requested payment amount. Once the transaction is submitted, the payment is complete.

Traceabletransactions

Bitcoin is completely transparent. All Bitcoin transactions are public, traceable and permanently stored on the Bitcoin network.

Bitcoin addresses are the only information used to define where Bitcoins are allocated and where they are sent.

These addresses are created privately from each user's folders. Since users normally have to reveal their identity to receive services or goods, Bitcoin addresses cannot remain anonymous. The Bitcoin network is a peer-to-peer network, and it is possible to record the user's IP addresses.

Countries that accept Bitcoin

The legal situation varies from country to country, but the list of countries that accept BTC is constantly expanding.

Bitcoin operates independently of any central bank, unlike other currencies such as US dollar and Euro.

The Bitcoin network has no other central point or administrator, which makes it a decentralized digital currency.

The fundamental value of Bitcoin is generated through "mining" and is closely linked to the costs of electricity and hardware, while the rest of its value is driven by its limited quantity, slow generation process and increasing demand.

Bitcoin is spreading around the world as a valid payment method for which various goods and services can be purchased; which is driving demand further.

Legality

Regulations vary from country to country. At the moment, only Japan officially recognizes Bitcoin as money, while in other countries there is still no specific legislation.

But domestic financial regulators can be expected to be increasingly interested in Bitcoin and other cryptocurrencies as blocking technologies are spreading rapidly and the size of this economy is growing.

Bitcoin Trading

Bitcoin is a volatile asset, with daily price changes of over 10%, making it highly risky for investing and trading.

Of course, there is no high reward without high risk and it is vital that you do not invest or use funds that you cannot afford to lose.

The causes of the collapse of Bitcoin in 2018

Over the course of 2017, the cryptocurrency market increased by 2000%. However, in 2018 the trend reversed and collapsed.

This led toa capitalization loss of approximately $700 billion. One of the advantages of CFD bitcoin trading is that the trader can trade going short and thus take advantage of the bearish trend.

The causes of the collapse were:

- ICO offers;

- money laundry;

- tax evasion;

- computer theft;

- market evolution;

- low or non-existent regulation in some cases;

- excessive speculation;

- investing in Bitcoins without buying them – CFDs.

Trading Bitcoin CFDs is probably not that different from trading any other currency pair, product or CFD that shows a strong trend.

The beauty of trading lies in its diversity, and through studies of price shares, traders should be able to make profits that make them financially independent and stable. So let's see how to trade with Bitcoin.

Bitcoin CFD traders should focus on:

- follow the trend (bullish trend until proven otherwise);

- proper money management;

- the main sessions London, New York and Tokyo;

- buying on BTC/USD price drops is important because it gives traders the opportunity to enter most of the market and follow the momentum. Of course, the trend will change, but BTC/USD is showing an exceptionally strong trend right now.

Proper money management is the holy grail of bitcoin trading, and if applied correctly in a strong trending environment, it should theoretically generate huge ROI.

CHAPTER NINE

RIPPLE

Most of the world's population has already heard of Bitcoin since its explosion in 2017, but the cryptocurrency family extends far beyond that. Those who have explored the topic a little more may have also heard of Litecoin and Ethereum.

Another cryptocurrency that has caused ripple effects across the digital currency market is Ripple. Even though Ripple has its own currency, its value is perhaps more considerable thanks to the ultra-fast payment system that supports it.

Ripple is a company born in San Francisco from the design of a payment system similar to the blockchain system. It is a protocol that works similar to a payment system, a remittance network, and currency exchange. It works with cryptocurrencies, fiat coins and commodities.

Ripple allows customers to integrate the protocol into their systems. National Bank of Abu Dhabi has recently started using blockchain technology for some of its transactions, such as international transactions. This allows its clients to transfer funds of various amounts virtually in real time.

Ripple uses a Bitcoin-like blockchain, but Ripple's cryptography is called "Ripples".

In terms of market capitalization, Ripple is the third largest cryptocurrency - after Bitcoin and Ethereum.

The abbreviation for Ripple is simply XRP. It can also be paired with other currencies, as well as USD (US dollar) and EUR (Euro).

The name of the currency pair Ripples vs. US dollar is therefore XRP/USD.

Ripple VS Bitcoin

Ripple is considered a competitor to Bitcoin and has some advantages over its more famous "cousin". Ripple does not depend on a single company to secure and manage their transaction database. Therefore, there is no waiting for block confirmations. According to Market Mogul, there is a difference between the time of liquidation of Bitcoin and Ripple. Bitcoin's settling time increased, reaching 168 minutes on March 27, 2018, while Ripple took an average of 3.7 seconds. Money transfers between Spain and Mexico made by BBVA revealed that Ripple takes only seconds, while a standard wire transfer would have taken four days.

Both currencies share many similar characteristics, and Ripple is similar to Bitcoin crypto with a few differences:

- Ripple offers faster settlement time,as explained above;

- Ripple uses an iterative consensus process,Bitcoin uses so-called mining;

- Currency vs. Network Transactions: Bitcoin is a decentralized digital currency, while Ripple is basically a transaction network that also includes a digital currency.

You cannot mine with Ripple. The Ripple cryptocurrency was born with a fixed number of Ripples (XRP) and has no expansion built into it, according to the rules of the Ripple protocol. Therefore, there is no need to mine new coins.

The total number of XRPs created is 100 billion, but the flow of XRP is controlled by Ripple. This has been criticized by Bitcoin sympathizers who praise Bitcoin for not being centralized on its creation or distribution.

Ripple responded announcing its intention to freeze 88% of its XRP assets and sell one billion XRP each month. Both freezing and constant flow will allow ripple traders and investors to have some level of predictability with respect to supply.

Ripple emphasizes its role in the "global settlement network", which simply allows financial parties, such as banks, to reduce transaction costs. At the same time, it also offers an advanced service with direct and instant transactions. The image below shows how Ripple allows payments to cross the world in the blink of an eye.

Payments are cryptographically secure and designed to fit into a bank's existing infrastructure. Ripple highlights the following four main features:

- distribution: banks can deal directly with each other without intermediaries;

- security: confidentiality of transactions;

- scalability: high levels of processing;

- interoperability: ability to connect multiple networks together.

The network for investing in Ripple allows you to complete payments faster (almost instantaneously) and cheaper, safer and with direct access. It's no surprise, then, that Ripple is increasingly being used by the banking sector, which hasn't capitalized as much on new technologies as some other sectors of the industry.

Blockchain

Ripple uses a structure that processes payments in a similar way to the concept of blockchain. It is a "storage ledger" for processing transactions that allows you to work across borders and with any payment size.

Ripple cryptocurrency helps facilitate transactions between two parties if direct exchange is not possible and has no counterparty risk as it is not dependent on third parties.

Investingin Ripple

Ripple is believed to have been founded by Ryan Fugger, but has seen a great deal of development since its initial creation.

Ripple's growth began in 2004 when the creation of RipplePay was founded by Ryan Fugger. In 2011, the system was redesigned, making it faster and much more efficient than Bitcoin. In 2012, OpenCoin, Inc. was formed.

Soon after, the Ripple Transaction Protocol (RTXP) was developed based on Fugger's concepts. The protocol is able to process the commissions and waiting times of the corresponding traditional banking system.

Since 2012, Ripple has also focused on expanding the banking market.

In short, the future for this financial product looks bright. Ripple's network is much faster at processing payments than its competitors and is aligning multiple partnerships with global companies:

- 60 institutions from around the world, including famous companies such as UBS, RBC, UniCredit and Santander;

- 40% of Japanese banks will be linked to Ripple;

- RBS and BAML will use Ripple for both retail and commercial payment services from 2018;

- Abu Dhabi National Bank uses Ripple for international transactions.

Of course, Ripple isn't as popular as Bitcoin. However, with the growing interest in cryptocurrencies in general, in addition toRipple's amazing fast network and ability to offer payment solutions, it looks like it will be a big contender for the market leader in the coming years. The volume division for XRP is shown below.

Ripple operates independently of any central bank in a similar way to other cryptocurrencies, such as Bitcoin, Ethereum and Litecoin. This is a major difference

from well-known currencies such as US dollar and Euro. These coins are distributed and printed in the US and EU by their respective central banks.

Ripple decides the flow of XRP, which is set at one billion XRP every month. However, unlike "fiduciary currencies" like USD and EUR, Ripple has a maximum supply of 100 billion XRP, which is available under the protocol.

Risks of Investing in Ripple

As with any financial asset, there is a risk that the price will go up and down. Ripple is subject to market fluctuations, such as supply and demand. However, price fluctuation is what allows traders to trade Ripple.

Considering the great acceptance of Ripple as a financial network by both major banks and many financial companies, it is unlikely that major disruptions will occur in the future.

Last but not least, each Ripple account must have a minimum reserve of 20 XRP and a transaction fee of 0.00001 XRP for each trade. These actions are designed to limit hackers who intentionally want to overload the network. In general, these ground rules are not heavy.

It is legal to invest in Ripple. Regulations vary in detail from one country to another, but the general expectation is that national financial regulators are interested in investing in Ripple and other cryptocurrencies.

For example, a law has already been passed in Japan to normalize and regulate digital currencies such as Bitcoin and XRP.

Investing in Ripple is as safe as using Bitcoin, Litecoin,Ethereum, or any other product. We suggest trading the XRP vs USD pair.

Most traders prefer trading on the Forex and CFD market, but cryptocurrencies offer a wide mix of tradable instruments.

Invest in Ripple Successfully

Operating in a shorter period of time always requires more practice and experience than operating in longer periods of time. Yes, there are more trading opportunities when investing in the 15 minute chart, but there is also more confusion and traders need to be more critical with the settings they choose.

In trading based on technical analysis you should always check if there is a possible news event or data release that could lead to spontaneous and rapid price increases. We are fundamentally cautious at these times andwe prefer to trade with normal trends rather than sudden price spikes. In particular, technical traders want to trade technically andto avoid price movements based on specific events.

The next step when trading shorter time slots and daily trades with XRP/USD is to consider the direction of the broader trend. This is one of the main reasons why we have added the 144 EMA near the chart.

The price must be above the EMA before trading any of the intraday setups.

If the price is below the EMA, we will omit any intraday settings.

After that we will look for long trades that are based on break or bounce settings when using trend lines and MT4 Pivot Points.

The trendline is a dynamic tool that traders need to draw on the chart.

Pivot Points are automatically added to static support and resistance levels.

Both Pivot Point (PP) indicators and trend lines can be used for pause and bounce settings:a pulse above the trendline or PP is an interruption pattern, a return on the trend line or PP is a rebound configuration.

Of course, this is just a rough idea of how to approach intraday trading. There are many different types of trading methods that could be used to enter the markets. You can find other articles that delve into various trading strategies in our educational section.

It is possible to make a profit in trading Ripple but it is always important to realize that trading involves risk, which means that you can lose money. There are a couple of key elements that you must always keep in mind when trying to make money trading in the markets.

It is important to keep in mind that trading requires patience and discipline. This is the "trading psychology" part and it is an important aspect to remember before entering the markets. If you don't, you may be tempted to trade forthe"payback", negotiateand analyze more than you should, and/or suffer other traps that lead traders to lose habits and false prejudices and turn this into a casino.

The other key aspect is risk management. When traders take a lot of risks, it becomes a gamble and the possibility of losing all trading capital increases. It is possible that this situation will degenerate over time. To avoid losing all trading capital, each trade should be divided into small amounts of capital, such as 0.5%, 1% or 2%. A period of losses will generally not lead to a significant decrease in the account and will allow traders to continue investing for another day.

Last but not least, traders must approach the markets with a solid trading plan that indicates how to analyze the charts, how to trade, manage settings and exit the market. Each trader has their own strategy and prefers different types of tools and indicators. This is why it is important to practice your trading plan first on a demo account or a real account with little risk.

Excitement for Ripple grew when a new high against the US dollar was reached on May 17, 2017. The price action took a steep rise, but that moment was an unsustainable energy explosion in the long run. The price has corrected as the markets do.

CHAPTER TEN

DASH

The cryptocurrency Dash was first released in 2014. This open source cryptocurrency offers simple and scalable solutions. Open source means that technology and software are created, tested and improved with the collaboration of users.

The Dash is the first fully decentralized digital money system and is increasingly accepted by companies on the Internet. Dash allows you to make instant and private payments online, as well as in physical stores. Being a "Blue Chip", you can get the Dash (cryptocurrency) in most exchanges.

Dash cryptocurrency is another alternative to decentralized digital currency.

It is a type of open source Peer-to-Peer cryptocurrency that offers features similar to Bitcoin but with some more advanced features, such as InstantSend instant transactions and PrivateSend transactions which we will explain later.

It should be noted that Dash is the first decentralized autonomous organization and that it uses two layers in its architecture to lead the network.

On the one hand we have the first level with the miners who are responsible for the security of the network and where the transactions are recorded in the blockchain, and on the other hand we have the second level consisting of "Masternodes" which make it possible for the crypto dashboard from Dash to enjoy advanced features.

Dash first appeared in January 2014, it started being called XCoin using the XCO code, a month later it was called Daskcoin but it wasn't quite convincing. In the third month, in March, it was in fact changed to Dash, which is the name we know it by today.

Dash is a play on words that stands for "Digital Cash", that is digital money.

In the first two days of the launch, 1.9 million coins were minted, which represents about a quarter of Dash's current issue.

According to CoinmarketCap, in June 2017 the daily volume of Dash was about $100 million per day and market capitalization exceeded $1.4 billion.

Dash shares many features with Bitcoin and other major cryptocurrencies. The main point in common is the ability to send cash digitally over the Internet.

However, there are also some differences between Dash and Bitcoin including speed, cost, and governance. In all these aspects, the Dash is better positioned than the rest of the cryptocurrencies.

But without a doubt, the main advantage and difference between the cryptocurrency Dash and the Bitcoin is privacy. Both currencies operate through blockchains that allow financial transactions to be carried out without intermediaries.

Like Bitcoin, the cryptocurrency Dash guarantees anonymity as it is not obliged to reveal personal information (name, address). However, the big difference is that the solid coding of the Dash blockchain prevents the tracking of your transactions and thus ensures anonymity.

A Valid Alternative to Bitcoin

The Dash managed to improve the original idea of Bitcoin in terms of speed, cost and governance. Let's review these three crucial points one at a time.

Speed

The transaction speed between Dash and Bitcoin is not comparable. Confirming Bitcoin transactions can take more than 10 minutes. The Dash (cryptocurrency) completes a similar transaction in just 4 seconds. The speed difference is amazing.

Costs

Bitcoin transaction fees are around $6. The Dash reduced this rate to less than half a US dollar. However, Dash cryptocurrency fees are expected to increase in line with revenue.

<u>Governance</u>

The Dash demonstrates how changes in currency development can be incorporated without the need for hard forks or bifurcations. The concept of hard fork refers to the implementation of two different solutions. Bitcoin has incorporated several hard forks in its development. Bitcoin Cash is an example of a currency separating from its main currency, Bitcoin. The Dash manages this type of process through a voting system, which accelerates the implementation of changes.

How the Dash is issued

The issuance of new Dash cryptocurrency coins occurs through a process of mining. This process is the most common way of crypto coins to reward users who record transactions in the blockchain. The time it takes for the Dash to "pull" a block is less than two and a half minutes.

The newly issued Dash cryptocurrency coins are divided into three groups: miners: about 45% of new coins are given to miners to encourage high electronic participation in the blockchain process;

- masternodes: they also receive about 45% of the new number;

- development team: the remaining 10% is used to finance and support the marketing, customer service and development team.

You may not know the terms miners and masternodes, so let's see what they mean!

What are masternodes

Masternodes are based on the Proof-of-Stake (PoS) algorithm, a concept that allows the user to mine or validate transactions in bulk based on the amount of coins in their possession.

Bitcoin, for example, is based on the concept of Proof of Work (PoW). This implies that its blockchain must be validated by all nodes on the network.

The difference between masternodes and standard nodes is that the former reduce the number of nodes required to validate to carry out a transaction. This makes the total number of nodes manageable and solves transaction scalability problems.

As an economic incentive for their work, masternodes receive 45% of the new cryptocurrencies issued. Governance also has an impact on the future direction and course of the currency.

Unlike minors, masternodes don't need to protect the network via PoW, but they use secondary functions like PrivateSend, InstantSend and the governance functions we talked about above.

PrivateSend and InstantSend functions

PrivateSend and InstantSend are two additional functions of the Dash, which are based on the management masternodes. These functions have the following advantages;InstantSend allows you to sendtransfers in less than a second, while PrivateSend hides the details of the transfer and information about the sender and recipient. This is made possible by the fact that this feature mixes all transactions, making traceability difficult.

How the price moves

Between 2014 and 2016, the change in the price of cryptocurrencies was reduced. Since 2017, the price has taken off and volatility has risen tremendously, thenthe price fell sharply.

The Dash crossed the magical $100 line in March 2017. This first bullish move was just the beginning, reaching $200 in May to reach $400 in August. Over the next three months, the price remained at a range of $250 to $400, until the wide range of cryptocurrencies caused a spike.

In November 2017, the price continued to rise until it stopped at around $1600. This was its highest peak since then, the value of the cryptocurrency from Dash maintained a downtrend to reach $175 in June 2019.

Opinions

The advantages of Dash in terms of speed, cost, privacy and governance have given this cryptocurrency a solid niche in this new world of financial products. However, we think we have to wait a little longer to see if it can be extended.

Zcash

Zcash is a cryptocurrency that was born at the end of October 2016, and was listed at 33 Bitcoins in the first minutes of the negotiations.

The Zcash cryptocurrency automatically hides the identity of senders and recipients, as well as the amount of all transactions we carry out in its blockchain. Only those with a view key will be able to see the content of the operations.

Zcash is based on peer-reviewed cryptographic research. It has been programmed by a team of IT security engineers on an open-source platform. The whole programming has been based on the proven code of Bitcoin. Zcash uses advanced digital-cryptographic techniques, as "zero knowledge tests". The goal of this technique is to ensure the validity of transactions without showing additional information about them.

This algorithm is called zero-knowledge proofs and allows the creator of the transaction to include a validity test in it, without the need to transmit any information other than the fact that the transaction is true. In other words, no information is transmitted that anyone can read.

You can receive, store and spend money while showing transactions to only chosen parties, instead of showing transactions to everyone on the Internet. This is a big difference with Bitcoin and Ethereum, which cannot function without exposing all of their transactions to anyone on the Internet.

After debuting on the currency trading platforms in October 2016, the Zcash reached $1,000 per unit, rising to the level of the pioneer Bitcoin, currently around $100. Zcash is attracting the interest of Russian, Chinese, Venezuelan and Brazilian consumers. In Brazil, the currency is also used to pay taxes and utility bills. A maximum production of 21 million units is expected.

User privacy protection is precisely what sets it apart. But this opacity is, as expected, in the spotlight: it does not offer the transparency required by the authorities seeking to prevent it from being used for money laundering, terrorist financing, tax evasion or fraud. Zooko Wilcox, CEO of Zerocoin Electric Coin Company, which operates Zcash, hopes this feature will help companies overcome reluctance to use their currency as a reliable alternative to traditional state-controlled ones.

CHAPTER ELEVEN

ETHEREUM

Ethereum (ETH) is an open-source software platform based on blockchain technology, which allows developers to build and release decentralized applications. It is actually much more than a cryptocurrency, which is only a part of Ethereum's offering.

Bitcoin and Ethereumareboth built using distributed public network technology - known as blockchain. All their other features are different.

Bitcoin offers a single application - a peer-to-peer digital currency system that allows online payments. It is basically a coin in its essential form.

While Bitcoin uses blockchain technology to track who owns Bitcoins, Ethereum uses blockchain as a platform for running almost any decentralized application. Bloomberg once described it as "shared software that can be used by everyone but is tamper-proof". So the possibilities are truly endless!

Where does ethereum come from and who is its founder

Ethereum was originally created by VitalikButerin, a cryptocurrency researcher and programmer who previously worked on Bitcoin in 2013. An online crowdfunding done in 2014 was the key part of the platform's funding. The system went into operation on July 30, 2015, and was populated by 11.5 million "coins" ready for pre-sale.

How Ethereum works

In the Ethereum blockchain, instead of "mining" as with Bitcoin, users work to earn "Ether", a type of cryptocurrency that powers the wider network. In addition to being a tradable cryptocurrency, Ether is also used by developers to pay for services on the Ethereum network.

Investing in Ethereum CFDs and other cryptocurrencies without risk

The best way to practice cryptocurrency CFD trading is to open a free demo trading account. Both beginner and advanced traders can start from a demo account. This provides the entire live trading experience, including all the real-time information and analysis from the live markets, even without using your capital.

History of Ethereum

Since Ethereum's inception in 2015, its cryptocurrency, Ether has shown slow progress in its first year. But 2017 was a completely different story. The cryptocurrency started the year with a meager pricing of $7.76, and by the end of the year it was over $700, an increase of over 9000%! Unlike Bitcoin, that set its record at the end of 2017, Ethereumwas at his top in January 2018, reaching a peak of over $ 1300 in mid-January.

As with other cryptocurrencies, however, 2018 proved to be a test year for Ether, and its price has progressively declined since then, settling around $130 towards the end of the year. 2019 saw a first upward phase, peaking on June 26 at 361.61, and then returning to decline, closing the year at 127.55. The first month of 2020 the price resumed an uptrend.

As the public has become more and more informed about how to trade Ethereum and Bitcoin, more interest has been generated. The case of the Aether is even more interesting. It had a steep price hike almost exclusively because it is very much like Bitcoin, and investors wanted to jump on the boat early when prices were moderately low.

Of course, as with all markets, what goes up can go down. As well as 2017's fantastic gains were driven by some sort of multiplier effect of rising prices that pushed investor demand, which in turn pushed prices higher, thus triggering higher demand once the market started selling out in 2018, we saw a reverse reaction. A correction in investor demand frightened by prices, which has led to an increase in sales, driving prices down and thus further holding back demand.

Investingin Ethereum

The first half of 2019 got off to a good start for Ether investors, with prices exceeding USD 350 at one point. But in the second half of the year, the cryptocurrency returned most of these gains but still holds more than 15% above its annual opening price in November 2019.

While trading is currently in neutral mode, a break below USD 150 could clearly be considered a bearish signal and lead to a decline towards and even significantly below the psychological important level at USD 100 in 2020.

In any case, given the current situation of uncertainty due to the coronavirus pandemic, we recommend that you always keep yourself updated on the latest economic and financial news before making any investment.

Recommended strategies to invest in Ethereum

Technical trading and proven tools should be applied to the chart when trading Ethereum, which in turn could be a good basis for successful trading Ether CFD against the US Dollar. Considering its volatility, scalping strategies should be applied in intraday trading.

Those looking to trade ETH/USD need to prepare for some price instability, where steady profits could turn into losses in a split second.

A "flash crash" occurred on June 21, 2017, when the price dropped from around $320 to 10 cents. He recovered later, but investors and traders certainly took a hit during that time. Mr. Adam White, Vice President of GDAX, explained that an investor placed a multimillion-dollar short selling Ether order at 12:30 pm on Wednesday. The size of the order caused a drop in the price of the currency (which was already volatile).

As is well known, when the price reaches the stop loss, it creates additional momentum and potentially strong movement in a very short amount of time.Each closing of a buy position is an automatic sell on the market and vice versa.

Trading with ETHEREUM/USD

Proper money management is the foundation of any trader's success or failure. When used correctly in high trend cases, it can produce a great return on investment (ROI).Due to the high volatility, losses may also occur, so it is extremely important to use proper money management. Market stability could be achieved when power shifts from investors looking to profit from price fluctuations, to consumers actually using cryptocurrencies.

When that happens, volatility should stabilize. Traders should treat crypto trading the same way they would treat any investment in the initial start-up phase. Furthermore, intraday traders should definitely focus on the most important trading sessions, as the major trading centers provide the highest volatility in ETH/USD.

Fortunately, the MetaTrader 4 (MT4) platform offers the tool during the main market sessions - 24/5.

Bitcoin VS Ethereum

In 2017, the Ether was very hot. The sentiment towards Etherum was very positive at that time.

Of course, some of this sentiment has cooled along with the decline in the value of the ETH/USD CFD pair from its 2017 highs. It is a general truth, however, that sentiment will decline for any market that has undergone a severe value correction.

There are investors who believe that cryptocurrency prices will recover. One factor in Ethereum's favor is the potential of its platform, and in 2019 we started to see signs of institutional adoption of the technology.

Banking giant JP Morgan made headlines in early 2019 when it launched its JPM coin, which was touted as the first cryptocurrency backed by a US bank. While many news outlets have acknowledged that this new digital token uses blockchain technology, what many have not mentioned is that JPM's proprietary Quromblackchain is actually an enterprise-grade version of Ethereum. Where all this will actually lead is far from clear, of course, but this kind of concrete example of real use of Ethereum technology could serve to rekindle confidence.

That said, we must point out that the vast majority of Ethereum trading and cryptocurrency trading in general is pure speculation, and the current utility value for users is close to zero. Not many people use blockchain protocols, unlike many people who trade crypto. We may also see regulations coming in terms of trading, issuing and holding new currencies in the near future.

In 2018, the bubble burst and both currencies saw their price plummet, but never reached historical lows. 2019 saw an interesting new increase for Bitcoin, which was also reflected in the chart of those who had decided to invest in Ethereum, but with much less intensity.

In early 2020, Bitcoin nearly skyrocketed against the US dollar driven by uncertainty in traditional markets as many investors view it as a safe haven asset. Despite this, BTC collapsed coinciding with the stock market crash in mid-March when several European governments decreed the confinement of their citizens and the closure of economic activity following the Covid-19 pandemic.

Bitcoin was close to $5,000 as investors preferred to turn to traditional safe haven markets such as gold. At the end of June 2020, the most valuable cryptocurrency on the market recouped what was lost at the beginning of the year exceeding $9,000, according to the Coinmarketcap website.

Ethereum took a similar path in its price movement against the USD. ETH/USD was worth $7.65 on January 1, 2017 and a year later it was above $1,300. Between 2018 and 2019, like Bitcoin, its price plummeted and sometimes even dropped to $100. In 2020, Ethereum's chart was similar to Bitcoin, bouncing to around250USD in February, falling in mid-March to 106 USDand recovering what was lost in the following months, to USD 244 at the end of June.

Who will have the best results in the future? This is very difficult to say, but Bitcoin's leadership role could give Bitcoin a bullish continuation, and reach new highs. It is likely that the highest Bitcoin price has not yet been quoted.

From this point of view, the Bitcoin chart seems to have the advantage, as it is considered the market favorite. The difference is clearly seen when compared to Ethereum, which although it has had its rallies, it does not move the same volumes.

However, both instruments have risen and decreased a lot over the past three years, so keep in mind that there is always a risk that prices will move sharply in the face of unexpected news.

Each cryptocurrency has a different method and set of rules that go hand in hand with its creation, distribution and protection or security. It is useful to know the details of each cryptocurrency, whether it is Bitcoin or Ethereum trading, the important thing is to be comfortable with its parameters.

There are several fundamental differences between the two cryptocurrencies, below hereare a couple of examples to understand if bitcoin or ethereum is better.

The Bitcoin supply is limited to a maximum of 21 million, while the Ethereum supply has limited growth every year.

Bitcoin was created in 2009 and has a block time of 10 minutes, while in Ether it is around 14 seconds.

It's not mandatory to trade an instrument you like, but having faith in its long-term potential and design could make it easier to invest in Ethereum or Bitcoin and aim for bigger goals. This particular factor is very personal and depends on each trader.

Bitcoin remains the best known cryptocurrency and seems to be no threat that it could lose that position. Therefore, the possibility that Bitcoin will be able to maintain this status over the next few years is entirely acceptable.

The advantage of Bitcoin's leadership role is that it could attract more investors. Cryptocurrencies in general, but Bitcoin specifically, may be increasingly attractive to large investors, perhaps even institutional investors. Bitcoin is well positioned to receive even more attention than in the past, Ethereum may receive a lower volume of investment, but this remains to be seen.

Bystaying abreast of certain developments within each cryptocurrency, you also gain key insights into possible price reactions. For example, the Bitcoin Cash hard fork, far from the original Bitcoin, had a temporary impact on prices, so tracking trends like this can be important.

From this point of view, Ethereum is slightly more stable than

Bitcoin, taking into account the most recent split. Either way, it doesn't hurt to monitor each cryptocurrency's latest trends and see if either of them offers less risk and more stability. This too can change from month to month, as the trends and news updates in this space continue to be dense and fast.

Trading is not only based on long-term potential or fundamentals, but also on the volatility and price actionof a cryptocurrency. This is especially important when trading Ethereum or Bitcoin in shorter time periods for example.

Slow moving instruments do not offer attractive trading setups because it is difficult to make a profit by entering and exiting if the price goes up or down. Volatility is the key, as it offers more opportunities for traders.

Price action is alsofundamental- it is important to review Ethereum or Bitcoin trading charts and familiarize yourself with the tool. This is even more true for short-term charts, where price action can sometimes be quick and unexpected. Some tools also fit your trading style more naturally. You should always make sure you know how to trade Bitcoin CFDs before trading with real money.

CHAPTER TWELVE

HALVING BITCOIN

2020 was a historic year for financial markets, with all types of assets experiencing great market volatility and extraordinary price changes. However, it will be this May 2020 that will shake up the cryptocurrency market.

The "Halving Bitcoin" event predicts that production of this digital currency will be reduced by 50%. This event is written in the rules of the underlying Bitcoin code with no one in control of the process, creating unique trading opportunities to know this tool and its properties well.

Halving Bitcoin

Bitcoin's unique digital design predicts that every four years there is a seismic shift in the cryptocurrency. For the third time in 11 years of history, in May 2020 it will undergo another major change.

To understand the halving of Bitcoin it is important to understand the basic principles of Bitcoin itself.

The code predicts that only 21 million Bitcoins can be produced. About 18 million Bitcoins have already been produced through the so-called "crypto-mining". Bitcoin mining is abig business where miners use high specification computers to help process Bitcoin transactions. These transactions are added as "blocks" to the blockchain ledger, which is the technology behind cryptomination.

The miners doing this work need considerable computing power, which comes at a cost. That is why when a block is added to the blockchain, the miner who worked it is compensated with Bitcoins, also known as a "miner's grant" or "block grant".

This is also how new Bitcoins are added to the supply chain, as a fixed amount of new Bitcoins are released in each bulk transaction. Miners can sell their earned bitcoins through an exchange.

The Bitcoin halving refers to the 50% reduction in compensation to the miners who maintain the Bitcoin network. What excites traders and investors the most is what could happen to the Bitcoin price during this period.

When and how it will happen

The Bitcoin halving is performed, as we anticipated, about once every four years or whenever 210,000 blocks are mined. The halving in May 2020 will take place in block 630,000. Although blocks are added to the blockchain approximately every 10 minutes, the exact date and time can be difficult to pinpoint, as the compound effect of small variations can make a big difference.

Many analysts predicted that Bitcoin's halving would likely take place between May 10-12. It looks like it will be like this.

According to the most accurate estimates, the 2020 bitcoin having will be on May 12th.

This halving will drop the miner's rewards from 12.5 bitcoins per block to 6.25 bitcoins.

When Bitcoin was first released, the reward for the miner was 50 bitcoins.On November 28, 2012, the amount dropped to 25 bitcoins.On July 9, 2016, it dropped to 12.5 bitcoin.

However, what excites most cryptocurrency traders, investors and enthusiasts is the fact that the amount of bitcoins entering the supply chain will be reduced while demand will remain at the same level. This shift in supply versus demand could help raise the price of the cryptocurrency.

Since Bitcoin halving has already happened twice in the past, let's take a look at the change in the price of bitcoin at that time.

While it is impossible to say for sure how prices will react to the 2020 Bitcoin halving, we can see how the Bitcoin price has reacted to previous bitcoins.

In both previous Bitcoin halvings, the price of bitcoin saw its value rise a year earlier and a year later. Both cases were in a general context of cryptocurrency market growth and global economic stability, which makes 2020 a very different year due to the impact of Covid-19.

Another important factor to remember is that this event is highly anticipated and therefore part of the potential increase in the value of bitcoin may already be included in the quoted price before the Bitcoin halving. However, to capitalize on any potential Bitcoin halvingmovement, it is essential to have the right tools in place.

A great way to get started is to open a free demo trading account to practice your trading ideas and strategies in a virtual environment until you feel ready to invest with real money. It is a great way to develop your skills until you are ready for a real trading account. Moreover, you'll have access to a variety of benefits, including free market analysis, access to advanced Trading Central indicators and tools, and much, much more.

CHAPTER THIRTEEN

HOW TO TRADE

Anyone who is minimally interested in learning about cryptography has taken part in some form of trading. As more and more attention is being paid, new participants want to enter the market and get their slice of crypto cake.

how to trade cryptocurrency

So, you have some money you want to invest. How do you intend to proceed? The portals that connect our world to the crypto worlds are called "exchanges". There are a lot of exchanges out there, but before you choose to invest in any of them, there are a few things you need to watch out for. Let's call it the "Exchange Checklist".

Validity

Before doing anything, first make sure that the exchange is available in your area. For example, Coinbase, one of the largest exchanges, is not available in India and Indonesia. So before you do anything, check this out.

Reputation

The next thing you need to check is the reputation of the exchange. Are people happy with their services? Has it been hacked recently?

How safe is it? Have people complained? Twitter and Reddit are great sources to check this out.

Exchange rates

The next step is exchange rates. Different exchanges have their own exchange rates which can vary. Do your homework here and look for 3 or 4 exchanges and their rates.

Security

Always choose exchanges that need an identity verification from you. While they may take some time, they are easily 100 times safer and more secure than anonymous exchanges. Ultimately, it's your hard earned money. You have to take an extra step to keep them safe.

How to start trading

To protect your cryptocurrency, you need to have a wallet. The wallet saves your private key and public address which helps you to store, send and receive cryptocurrencies. While this should be very clear to you, let's take a quick overview of the meaning of the private key and the public address:

- private key: the private key gives you the right to log in and send your money;

- public address: this is the address where everyone will send you money.

One thing to remember before continuing, the public address is what you will give others to send your money.

DO NOT and we repeat DO NOT give your private key. The private key is for you and you only. If you give your private key to strangers, they will have access to your money.

All crypto wallets fall into the following two categories:

- warm preservation;

- cold room.

Hot storage vs. cold storage

Before we go deeper, let's use an analogy to understand the difference between the two. The warm wallet is like the wallet you carry in your pocket. It gives you easy access to your money, but is quite vulnerable.

The cold room, on the other hand, is like your savings account. Highly impractical for everyday use, but extremely safe when comparing the two.

<u>Warm preservation</u>

An internet-connected wallet is called "hot storage". Below are some examples of hot wallets,but before we get to the heart of each of these wallets, let's look at the pros and cons of hot wallets.

Hot Wallets pros:

- it gives you quick, easy and immediate access to your funds;

- getting easy support in different devices;

- very easy to use and ideal for beginners.

Hot Walletscons:

- vulnerable to hackers and cybercrime;

- unless the keys have been carefully saved, if the device is damaged, the wallet will also be damaged;

- the device where the warm wallet is stored, such as the laptop, phone, etc. is also susceptible to physical theft.

So now that you have a general idea of what a Hot Wallet is, let's look at some of the more popular types.

Hot Wallet: exchange wallets

This is the simplest wallet you can ever create. In fact, if you followed our instructions and created your Coinbase account, guess what? You have already created your exchange wallet!

The benefits are obvious. It is already linked to your account and gives you quick and easy access for trading. In any case, this also means that you are vulnerable to attack. Remember that exchanges are a constant target for hackers. We recommend that you do not keep an important part of your cryptos in exchange portfolios, but only keep what you need for trading.

Hot Wallet: desktop wallets and mobile wallets

Desk wallets and mobile wallets have become increasingly popular. Desk wallets offer more security than exchange wallets. Their setup is also very simple. All you have to do is downloadingthe client to your laptop/desktop and you're done! MultiBit provides an excellent desktop wallet to store Bitcoins.

However, there is a problem with desk wallets. They are not the most flexible options. After all, wallets cannot be accessed from any other desktop, apart from the one where it was downloaded.

That's why, for more users who want flexibility, mobile wallets are a pretty affordable option. Setup is as simple as downloading an application to your phone. MyCelium is a pretty popular mobile wallet for both Android and iOS.

The problem with both of these wallets is that, being stored on an internet-connected device, they are vulnerable to viruses and hackers.

Hot Wallet: multi-brand wallet

Have you ever seen one of those old school lockers that require multiple keys to open? Or those treasure chests that need 3 or 4 people to be opened at the same time?

This will give you an idea of how multi-signature wallets or multi-sig wallets work. Most ICOs use multisig wallets to raise and hold their funds. So why would you want to use multisig wallets?

To protect against corruption: we have all heard stories of ICOs making millions of dollars in their sale to the crowd. What's stopping all these developers from taking the money and running away? Human greed is powerful, after all. In situations like these, it is much more prudent to accept funds in a multi-digit wallet, where all the money and power does not depend on a single human being.

More security and insurance: since the funds are in a multisig wallet, they will automatically be safer because they no longer depend on the whims of a single person. Moreover, if I send my money to an address with multisig wallets, I will also feel reassured that my funds are not being mishandled.

Cold room

While hot wallets offer great accessibility, the fact remains that they are extremely insecure. That is why it is more prudent to save most of the funds in a ColdWallet. A Cold Wallet is completely cut off from the internet, which automatically keeps it safe from hackers and viruses.

Examples of cold storage wallets include:

- hardware wallet;

- paper wallet.

Before learning how to set up each of these aspects, let's try to understand the pros and cons of refrigerated wallets.

Pros:

- 100% safe from hackers and viruses;

- a great place to store and safeguardyour coins for a long period of time.

Cons:

- extremely impractical for day to day transactions;

- it is not suitable for beginners;

- it is still vulnerable to human inattention.

Well, now that we've covered that, let's figure out how to set up Cold Wallets.

Cold room - Hardware Wallets

Hardware Wallets are physical devices where you can store your own encrypted currency.

The most common form of Hardware Wallet is the USB style which was advocated by the French company Ledger. The reasons that have brought so much popularity to Hardware Wallets are the security and storage capacity of a Cold Wallet. This makes transactions very simple. Basically, it works and nullifies the biggest drawback of Cold Wallets.

Pros of Hardware Wallets

As this is a cold wallet, your private key will be safe. Keys are stored in the secure area of a microcontroller and cannot be transferred outside the device

They are designed to be elegant and can be carried easily.

Transactions are extremely easy. All you have to do is enter your wallet and then follow the instructions provided to make your transactions. The wallets UI interface is very simple to use.

Extremely safe and secure. As for the writing, there have been no cases of hardware wallet hacking.

It has the ability to store multiple addresses for sending your funds.

The wallet is protected by a pincode, so even if it falls into the wrong hands, they will not be able to access your funds. By entering the wrong pin code 3 times, the wallet will be closed. In case of closure, it is still possible to recover the funds by following the details of the restoration.

Cons of Hardware Wallets

Like all products, these wallets can also have design flaws. Recently, a design flaw was discovered in Ledger which made it potentially vulnerable. Ledger has faced the problem ever since.

It is a real physical item, which means it can be stolen or damaged.

They are not the most versatile when it comes to storing cryptocurrencies. Trezor stores 10 types of coins, while Ledger stores about 23.

Finally, you will need to trust that the company that is creating your Hardware Wallet is ethical and will not try to interfere with the design of it. It calls for trust in an environment that should be trustless.

So, now that the pros and cons have been addressed, let's see how you can create it! Without doubt the two most popular Hardware Wallets in the world are Trezor and Ledger Nano S.

Trezor

Trezor is a Prague-based company that has made one of the simplest and easiest to use Hardware Wallets ever. It's really stupidly simple to use and the design is so sleek and light that you can take it anywhere. It is compatible with Windows, Mac and Linux and its use is simple, just plug it into your laptop and connect it with one of the following interfaces:

- My Trezor;

- Multibit;

- Electrum.

Ledger Nano S

Ledger, is a Paris-based company that has given the crypto community one of the most user-friendly, stylish and popular Hardware Wallets. They store all your data in a smartcard that keeps them safe from hackers. To use it, simply connect it to your laptop and connect it to one of the following interfaces:

- Mycelium;

- Electric;

- Green address;

- Greenbits;

- CoinKite;

- Copay;

- MyEtherWallet.

Cold room - Paper Wallets

Paper Wallets are often considered the safest way to store your cryptocurrency. The idea behind a Paper Wallet is very simple. You set up an offline wallet by following a few simple instructions and then simply print the private and public keys on a piece of paper. The keys will also be printed in the form of a QR code which you can scan to gain access to your funds.

So, the questions you need to ask yourself now are: do you need a

Paper Wallet?

The answeris:it depends.

Are you going to use your funds fairly regularly? Then no. Paper Wallets will be a nuisance when used this way. Then you better get yourself a hardware portfolio.

However, if you are planning to hold your funds for an extended period of time, then, without a shadow of a doubt, the Paper Wallet is the way to go.

CHAPTER FOURTEEN

TOP 10 CRYPTOCURRENCY INVESTORS

The popularity and values of cryptocurrencies today are undeniable.

Far from the initial skepticism of 2009, when Satoshi Nakamoto published the historic "White Paper" with which he presented Bitcoin, this and other cryptocurrencies have gained an important place in the contemporary financial world, and more and more products and services can be paid for with cryptocurrencies.

Although cryptocurrencies have had strong price fluctuations that may have raised some doubts among potential investors, the truth is that most of those who have opted to invest their money in cryptocurrencies have achieved good economic results.

This list ranges from those who have built great fortunes by investing and trading with cryptocurrencies, to others who have created some of the cryptocurrencies that are among the most popular today.

1. The first is Chris Larsen, co-founder of Ripple, American, a graduate of Stanford. He owns 17% of the company that controls 61 billion of the 100 billion XRP tokens that will be issued in total. His fortune in cryptocurrency is estimated at $7.5 billion.

2.Then, we have Joseph Lubin, a Canadian creator of ConsenSys, and co-founder of Ethereum, another cryptocurrency of the most used today. Lubin studied at Princeton and his fortune is estimated to be between 2 and 3 billion.

3. There are Winklevoss brothers (Tyler and Cameron) co-founders of Winklevoss Capital. They started investing in Bitcoin starting in 2012 and created the Gemini Exchange, which is widely recognized in the cryptocurrency world. His fortune is around $1 billion.

4. On this list, there is also Matthew Mellon, who passed away just as we are writing this article, who was a Bitcoin investor when the majority of the public still did not know about cryptocurrencies and who, after selling his Bitcoin had invested $2 million in Ripple, also obtaining a large capital gain from this investment. Now, after his death, the question iswho will take care of the Ripple package that was his property and that he had declared to keep stored in various Hardware Wallets in the name of different people and in various places in the United States.

5. In the world of cryptocurrencies, everyone knows about the CoinBase Exchange, whose mobile application is among the most downloaded in the United States. Its CEO is the American Brian Armstrong, who studied at Rice University and who,thanks largely to CoinBase, has brought his fortune to almost $1000 million.

6.Matthew Roszak is an American entrepreneur who initially made his fortune with several software companies before delving into the world of cryptocurrencies. His investments in cryptocurrency as well as his Tally Capital and Bloq projects have allowed him to build a fortune of about $900 million.

7. Another Canadian in the ranking is Anthony Di Iorio, who studied at Ryerson University and has invested in several cryptocurrencies, including Qtum, Verchain and ZCash. He is among the co-founders of Ethereum. His fortune exceeds $750 million.

8. An American Brock Pierce, administrator of the Bitcoin Foundation, was one of the first to bet on cryptocurrencies. During the first decade of the 21st century, he founded Internet Gaming Entertainment, a highly successful internet gaming platform. His fortune exceeds $700 million.

9. Another important name to list is Michael Novogratz, an American CEO of Galaxy Digital, one of the largest cryptocurrency trading houses on Wall Street, who firmly believed in the cryptocurrencies in which he has invested millions of dollarsand this has allowed to increase his fortune now estimated at around $700 million.

10. The list ends with the Chinese Changpeng Zhao, a graduate of McGill University, is also one of the brightest minds in cryptocurrencies. He has been involved in several cryptocurrency projects, including his most recent and already legendary, Binance, which appears out of nowhere in 2017 to become the world's largest exchange in less than a year. His fortune ranges from $1 to

$2 billion.

CHAPTER FIFTEEN

CRYPTOCURRENCY IN THE FUTURE

Web giants and central banks find them particularly interesting,but the Financial Action Task Force (the intergovernmental organisation founded at the initiative of the G7 to develop policies to combat money laundering) - fears that they may also be used in illegal contexts to promote money laundering and finance international terrorism. Cryptocurrency, which has been in use for more than ten years now, has various potentials but also numerous risks, about which we have not yet been able to shed any definitive light.

Blockchain and Cryptography: the ingredients of cryptocurrencies

Cryptocurrencies are valuable digital representations that use peer-to-peer technologies (i.e. between two devices directly, without the need for intermediaries) to purchase goods and services. The nodes of the networks are made up of computers that can potentially be distributed all over the world, on them are run special programs that perform coin purse functions. Transactions and release take place collectively on the network, so there is neither centralised management nor control authority.

The decentralised control of each cryptocurrency works through a blockchain, which acts as a database of public financial transactions. The blockchain consists of a constantly growing list of records, called blocks, which are linked and protected by encryption.

Bitcoin: the cryptocurrency of the mysterious nakamoto

There are over 6,000 cryptocurrencies in the world. The first to be known on a large scale, and perhaps the most famous, is Bitcoin. It was created in 2009 by a mysterious computer scientist whose only known alias, Satoshi Nakamoto. To date, a Bitcoin is worth just under 9 thousand euros, a value that it has maintained with some fluctuations over the past year. A limited number of Bitcoins are expected to be issued over the next few decades: 21 million units by 2140. Despite their popularity, the security of Bitcoins is not certain: the writing at the base of the blockchain could hide some imperfections easily exploitable by cyber criminals.

Ethereum and Altcoins

Over the years, other cryptocurrencies have emerged, Altcoins, which claim to offer users more advanced privacy and security requirements than their big sister. One of the best known is the Ethereum, born in 2015. It is able to securely digitize the conclusion of a wide variety of contracts: financial transactions, electoral systems, domain name registration, crowdfunding platforms, intellectual property and insurance. The main difference to Bitcoin is that the Ethereum is not only a network for the exchange of monetary value but a network that supports a multitude of transactions. Ethereum contracts pay for the use of its computing power through a cryptocurrency, Ether, which also has the function of supporting the platform. To date, an Ether is worth just under 300 euros, since its inception it has only exceeded 1000 euros in 2018.

Potentials and risks

After the financial crisis of 2008, cryptocurrencies have enjoyed considerable success, presenting themselves in the world of markets as the new way of giving and receiving guarantees in financial transactions. Buying them, however, is not for everyone; on the contrary, due to their volatility, cryptocurrencies are considered a high risk investment. As of today, cryptocurrencies cannot be considered currencies, but financial investments. They are not comparable to money for two reasons: first they are not a widespread and efficient payment instrument, the second reason is the instability of their value. As financial investments they have a high volatility, they can therefore please risk lovers and those who appreciate their presumed anonymity.

Anonymity: reality or utopia?

The standard blockchain we started to know with Nakamoto is not a totally anonymized system but a pseudo-anonymized one, it is in fact possible to trace Bitcoin flows very effectively and, consequently, to trace the transactions made to specific identities present in the system. As far as the legality of the transactions is concerned, everything depends on the type of platform on which it is traded. If someone wants to commit an offence, they can easily go to the Bitcoin: all they need to do is keeping away from regulated markets (platforms that group anonymous codes) that respect the rules of the countries where they operate and instead choose platforms that do not care about legality. In regulated markets, in fact, not only does the blockchain make it possible to trace transactions and discover offences, but market operators have the right to intervene and possibly notify the competent authorities of the country in question.

The Zuckerberg Libra and stablecoins

For some years now there has also been talk of Stablecoins, a new type of cryptocurrency. The most famous example is the Libra, launched in 2019 by Facebook creator Mark Zuckerberg. But the project is still frozen, while another Stablecoin, Gram, designed by Pavel Durov, died before it even saw the light, invalidated by the American Sec.

But how does this new generation of cryptocurrencies differ from the Bitcoin? In order to overcome the instability of the value of cryptocurrencies, some issuers promise to anchor the trend in a basket of existing coins or public financial assets. But how credible is this promise, given that we are not talking about sovereign states, but about private operators? Even Stablecoins remain bets. What is certain is that the Financial Action Task Force has sent a report on these new cryptocurrencies to the G20 finance ministers and national bank governors, which it is monitoring from 2014, in which it reiterates the risk that they will be used for money laundering.

Digital public coin

This year, however, following the digital opening imposed by the Covid emergency, central banks have become interested in the world of cryptocurrencies and are preparing to mint coins made of bits. According to the Bri (Banque des RèglementsInternationaux), 80% of the central banks are working on it, 40% have started experiments, 10% have set up pilot projects. The Fed is also carrying out research with the MIT on the subject and China launched a programme at the beginning of the year, in open challenge to the dominance of the dollar.

It is only a matter of time before the central banks will sooner or later have to produce digital public money. However, the issuance of this currency is a Pandora's box, because it opens up technical and political questions both in monetary policy and in banking and financial supervision. So we just have to wait.

CHAPTER SIXTEEN

LIBRA FACEBOOK

Libra is the cryptocurrency announced by Facebook in June 2019 and promises to revolutionize the universe of payments and financial transactions. His announcement aroused praise and consensus, but also doubts and criticisms. In the months following the launch, financial authorities around the world moved to verify the controversial aspects, some of the world's top economic and financial leaders expressed opposing positions and some of the organizations that initially supported Libra pulled back.

The latest in order of time is Vodafone: the company, initially among the supporters of the project, has made it known that the resources previously allocated to Libra will be redirected to its consolidated digital payment service M-Pesa, currently active in 6 African nations. To this day, many people fear that cryptocurrency will never see the light, despite Facebook, until recently, seemed willing to continue on its way. On the other hand, at the end of January Mark Zuckerberg announced the international launch of WhatsApp Pay, a payment system via chat. It is not yet clear how the new solution will fit into the "Facebook ecosystem" of payments. But let's see what Libra is and how it works, what has happened so far and what to expect from the future.

The Launch of Libra

"We want to make it easy for everyone to send and receive money just like our apps to share messages and photos" wrote founder and CEO Mark Zuckerberg on June 18, 2019 in a post on the social network with which he broke the news and provided additional details. The project, which should take off in 2020, is not limited to creating a new cryptocurrency but involves the development of an entire ecosystem: a global financial infrastructure accessible to billions of people. The initiative is governed by the Libra Association, a non-profit association based in Geneva, which currently includes about 20 members including companies, non-profit organizations and international academic institutions, but the goal is to reach 100 members by year. In the meantime, however, after the official announcement, Libra has come under pressure from many quarters, particularly over the issue of its regulation. In the first week of July, the US Federal Reserve declared that Facebook's plans to create a digital currency "cannot go on" until all controversial issues are clarified. The company initially responded that it relied on constructive dialogue. Then, at the beginning of August, Mark Zuckerberg, in a post, took a kind of backtrack, warning that Libra and its subsidiary Calibra could experience significant delays or even never be launched. A tactic to counter the pressure and criticism that rained down on him from many sides since he announced the Facebook cryptocurrency?

In the first week of July, the US Federal Reserve stated that Facebook's plans to create a digital currency "cannot go on" until all controversial issues are clarified. The company initially responded that it relied on constructive dialogue. Then, at the beginning of August, Mark Zuckerberg, in a post, took a sort of backtrack, warning that Libra and the subsidiary Calibra could experience significant delays or even never be launched. A tactic to counter the pressure and criticism that rained down on him from many sides since he announced the Facebook cryptocurrency? Or an authentic back-of-front?

One thing is certain: all the banks want to see this clearly. On September 16, representatives of the US Federal Reserve, the Bank of England and 24 other central banks met with representatives of the Libra project in the Swiss city of Basel to discuss how the blockchain will operate and the objectives pursued.

Libra's path seems increasingly uphill: at the end of September 2019 some relevant financial partners such as Visa and Mastercard began to review their involvement in Facebook's cryptocurrency, worried about the decisions that regulators will make. After that, in October 2019, Paypal, eBay, Visa, Mastercard and Booking definitively announced their defection. But in the meantime let's see what led to its birth and why.

On June 18, 2019, with a post on Facebook, the founder and CEO of the social network, Mark Zuckerberg, launched the new currency called Libra and at the same time the non-profit association of the same name together with other 28 international organizations around the world. The news had been anticipated the previous week, but for some time, at least for a couple of years, the Internet giant had been working on the operation. For the past year and a half, Facebook has had a fluctuating relationship with cryptocurrencies. On the one hand, it has shown interest, also leaking news on possible acquisitions in this area (for example, Coinbase, a well-known cryptocurrency exchange company). On the other hand, digital currency ads have often been blocked and banned on its platforms for long periods.

The turning point was a gesture by Zuckerberg that was passed over in silence by the media: in January 2018, it acquired a license in Ireland to offer personal loans to its 2.07 billion users. Then over the past six months the interest has gradually become more concrete with various rumors about the issue of a possible cryptocurrency by Facebook, until the official announcement.

Facebook has therefore officially entered the world of payments, more precisely in that of cryptocurrencies. The declared objective is to provide access to the financial system to the approximately 1.7 billion unbanked adults present in the world today, that is, all those who do not have a bank account or similar services.

The founding members

There are three key elements of the Libra project: the association of actors that governs it, the blockchain on which it is based and the cryptocurrency with which it is used. In short, Libra is a non-monolithic ecosystem, which brings together companies, associations and investors from different sectors for the first time. As for the association that governs the project, it is called Libra Association and it is a non-profit based in Geneva, which initially included 28 members including companies, non-profit and multilateral organizations, academic institutions from all over the world.

These organizations join the association by actively participating in the Libra network, running a validation node on the network, and serving in governance in exchange for rewards generated by transaction fees, conversion fees, and deposit interest.

The founding members who in June 2019 pledged to work for the development, dissemination and acceptance of the new cryptocurrency were:

- payments sector: Mastercard, PayPal, PayU (Naspers' fintech arm), Stripe, Visa;

- technology and marketplaces sector: Booking Holdings, eBay, Facebook/Calibra, Farfetch, Lyft, MercadoPago, Spotify AB, Uber Technologies, Inc. ;

- telecommunications sector: Iliad, Vodafone Group;

- blockchain sector: Anchorage, Bison Trails, Coinbase, Inc., Xapo Holdings Limited;

- venture capital sector: Andreessen Horowitz, Breakthrough Initiatives, Ribbit Capital, Thrive Capital,

Union Square Ventures;

- non profit and multilateral organizations, and academic institutions: Creative Destruction Lab, Kiva, Mercy Corps, Women's World Banking.

The conditions required to become a member must be at least two out of three of the following:

- value: more than $1 billion in market value or more than $500 million in customer account balances;

- scale: reaching more than 20 million people per year, in multiple countries;

- sustainability: to be recognized as Top-100 by third-party or media associations in the area of sustainability (e.g. by Interbrand Global 100, Fortune 500, the S&P Global 1200, the FTSE Eurotop 300).

Funding Members will be remunerated for their work. They will in fact be entitled to the Libra Investment Token, a second token of the platform, linked to the returns from the securities held by the Libra Reserve. Facebook apparently worked for over a year on a project which it then shared both governance and potential revenues with other players. The White Paper also talks about the future objective of further opening the network, even making it totally permessionless, consequently modifying the remuneration mechanism envisaged today. However, neither Apple, nor Google, nor Amazon, nor Microsoft are among the partners and there is no bank either. All technical information can be found on the website www.libra.org.

Founding members: the defections

The presence of the giants of the payment world, from Mastercard to Visa, from PayPal to Stripe, should have worked as a guarantee for the reliability of the project. Instead, between September and October 2019 these actors all abandoned. EBay and Booking, part of those hi-tech groups that should have adopted Libra as a payment tool, have also decided not to participate.

On October 14, The Libra Association formalized its board of directors and executive team, with CEO David Marcus (former blockchain Leader at Facebook). Of the initial 28 members who showed interest, 21 formally signed the statute of the Libra Association, the entity in charge of managing and governing the cryptocurrency blockchain architecture. The Association has seen the defections of Mastercard, VISA, Paypal, Mercado Pago, eBay, Stripe, Booking Holdings, leaving PayU as the only payment company at the moment.

In addition to the aforementioned David Marcus (Calibra), who was in charge of the project from the beginning, Matthew Davie (Kiva), Patrick Ellis (PayU), Katie Haun (Andreessen Horowitz) and WencesCasares (Xapo) were appointed to the board. The board then voted on the association's executive team consisting of Bertrand Perez, chief operating officer and president, Dante

Disparte, head of policy and communications and vice president, and Kurt Hemecker, head of business development.

At the same time, again on October 14, the association confirmed that it had received indications of interest from more than 1,500 counterparties, with 180 counterparties that meet the criteria required to become founding members. Objective: reaching100 members.

Vodafone also left the game on 22 January 2020. It was the eighth defection from the Libra Association: practically a third of the initial members left. Vodafone has declared its intention to concentrate its resources on the M-Pesa project, a system for the transfer of money and microcredit launched in 2007 by the subsidiary Safaricom, currently only available in some countries: Kenya, Tanzania, Afghanistan, South Africa, India, Romania and Albania. Now Vodafone would aim to expand M-Pesa to other countries.

How the Calibra Wallet Will Work

Libra is not the only entity that was revealed to the world on June 18. In fact, Calibra, a company directly controlled by Facebook, was also officially presented. Calibra is the first wallet available to manage the new cryptocurrency and transact through this digital currency. Its prerogative is to simplify the user experience with respect to the complex management of private keys and public keys which is instead normally provided in all blockchain platforms, including Libra.

Wallets are widely used by all cryptocurrency holders and it will be interesting to see if other wallets integrate the possibility of making transactions through Libra. However, Calibra will certainly be the only tool to be perfectly integrated with Whatsapp and Messenger, the main messaging platforms managed by Facebook, thus making the exchange of money as simple as sending a photo.

Calibra will also have the role of ensuring compliance with AML (Anti Money Laundering, Anti-Money Laundering) regulations and carrying out the KYC of users ("Know Your Customer", the recognition process used by companies to verify the identity of their customers) in compliance of the regulations in force. It will also open up new scenarios for digital identity management, potentially enabling an evolved "sign in with Facebook" button that can be used not only for registration on sites, but also for access to services that require KYC such as financial or insuranceones.

Similarities and Differences With Other Cryptocurrencies

Facebook's Libra is a cryptocurrency. But there are currently at least 2,238 cryptocurrencies in the world. What are the peculiarities of the digital currency that will be issued starting from 2020 by the social network of Mark Zuckerberg? Fabio Pezzotti,

Founder, CEO and President of Iconium Blockchain Ventures explains: "If we consider the degree of decentralization, in the case of the Libra project this is limited when compared to permissionless and open-source infrastructures such as Bitcoin and Ethereum with miners or nodes of the order of thousands, and in fact the minimum requirements imposed by the association are very restrictive (for example a minimum of $10 million investment) and can only be met by a few organizations in the world. In other words, unlike Bitcoin, Libra will be a permissioned platform. Each of the Libra Association members will own a validator node. In permissionless platforms such as Bitcoin and Ethereum, anyone can participate in the validation process, while in Libra the validators will be dozens of large international companies".

As for the blockchain used, Facebook first acquired the entire team of the ChainSpacestartup, to develop a blockchain capable of supporting 1000 transactions per second and create a new programming language known as "Move" to develop on it. Security is one of the key principles on which this language is developed, with which it will be possible to create new assets, logic and decentralized finance applications on Libra.

Libra cryptocurrency is guaranteed by a basket of fiat currencies (for now Euro, USD, GBP, Yen) which will allow it to have a stable value over time and allow consumers and merchants to overcome the volatility risks that today disadvantage cryptocurrencies as a means of payment. There will be no monetary policy, it is possible to generate new Libra by depositing fiat money and vice versa it is possible to burn Libra by withdrawing fiat money.

The arrival of Libra could definitively unmark the difference created between cryptocurrencies and private digital forms of value transfer Facebook's entry into the market has certainly attracted attention of many professionals and not. Finally, each of these assets is finding its position within the market: Bitcoin an attractive safe haven asset from a speculative point of view, Libra a currency to make payments and maybeother projects in an ever-expanding market.

Facebook Updates Its Digital Currency Project

Of the changes made to the original project listed in the White Paper, the main one aims to dispel the concerns of financial regulators that Libra may interfere with the national currencies and monetary policies of individual countries, thanks also to the fact that it can immediately reach apoolof 2.5 billion potential users, the number of Facebook subscribers to date. To achieve this, the system will now also offer single currency Stablecoins, in addition to the original Libra backed by a basket of currencies and debt securities, such as Librausd (USD), Libraeur (EUR), Libragbp (GBP) and Librasgd (SGD). This will allow people and businesses in regions whose local currencies have single-currency Stablecoins on the Libra network to directly access a Stablecoin in their own currency.

Single currency linked Stablecoins will be usable anywhere in the world. A key objective of the economic project of the Libra network is the trust in an efficient payment method. Each Stablecoin on the Libra network will be fully backed by a pool of high quality liquid assets and backed by a competitive network of exchanges that buy and sell each coin. This means that Libra owners should have a high degree of certainty that they can convert Libra into local currency, the White Paper states. Libra, therefore, now appears almost like a digital version of currencies.

Furthermore, the association, aware of the fact that several central banks are now moving to create their own digital currency, hopes that its system can be perfectly integrated with central bank digital currencies (CBDC) as soon as they are available.

Facebook asks Finma for approval

The Libra "2.0" project was presented for approval to Finma, the federal supervisory authority on financial markets in Switzerland, the country where the Libra Association is based.

CONCLUSION

If you are reading the conclusion, it means that you have reached the end of the book.

I hope it was a pleasant reading and the content was interesting.

I hope all of this hashelped to improve your way of trading in cryptocurrency, but not only that!

I have also tried to help you understand how important it is to have a trading plan, or understand what your goals are or how best to manage risk.

I also hope with this book you will discover the method to make your trading more profitable, but above all, thatyou will learn the tools to try to safeguard your capital.

As I always say, trading doesn't mean playingatthe casino.

Trading has become their job for many, and for some, the possibility that has allowed them to significantly increase their standard of living.

But behind all this there is study, preparation, discipline, organization and above all, never improvisation.

I wish you every success in trading and in other types of business, have a good life!